What People Are Saying About

Feminist Witchcraft

Arguing that witchcraft is inherently political, and that politics is about power, this gem of a book explores the many implications of a truly inclusive, feminist approach to witchcraft. Powerfully written, the author engages with the history and theory of feminist theology and feminist craft in a way that is accessible to all. I found myself, as a queer woman and thealogian, feeling affirmed and inspired on every page.

Kelle BanDea, M.Div, D.Min, author of *Modron; Meeting the Celtic Mother Goddess*

This is the book we have all been waiting for! Feminism and Witchcraft have been linked together since the early seventies' feminist movements in the US and UK. Today the long-awaited spotlight has finally thrown its truthful glare on the genocide of women during the so-called witchcraft trials in the Middle Ages – women now are proud to call themselves witches – thanks largely to the feminist movement. But how can you unite the largely political ideology of feminism and the spiritual path of witchcraft into a sacred practice? In this book, the author examines both elements of the title in detail, exploring ways to incorporate traditional elements of witchcraft, such as spell craft and ritual, with political action and, in doing so, starts healing the wounds of patriarchy. A well-crafted and researched book, which clearly illuminates Susan Harper as a powerful advocate for the modern witch.

Thea Prothero, author of *A Guide to Pilgrimage*

As an initiate in a witchcraft tradition rooted in feminism (and mentioned in this book), I was eager to read *Feminist Witchcraft* by Susan Harper. This book begins with the history of goddess spirituality movements and the complexity of defining 'one way' to practice. The following chapters expand beyond cis-focused early writings and beliefs to include and embrace nonbinary, transgender, and other identities in modern spaces. I appreciated the emphasis on feminist witchcraft as relational and political, helping readers see the value in non-hierarchical thinking. For those tired of the patriarchy's influence, *Feminist Witchcraft* can help dismantle that thinking while providing guidance for rituals, spellwork, and activism to inspire change within and without.

Irisanya Moon, Reclaiming Witch and author of *Artemis: Goddess of the Wild Hunt and Sovereign Heart, Circe: Goddess of Sorcery, Hestia: Goddess of Hearth, Home, and Community,* and many others

Pagan Portals

Feminist Witchcraft

Pagan Portals

Feminist Witchcraft

Susan Harper

MOON
BOOKS

London, UK

Washington, DC, USA

CollectiveInk

First published by Moon Books, 2025
Moon Books is an imprint of Collective Ink Ltd.,
Unit 11, Shepperton House, 89 Shepperton Road, London, N1 3DF
office@collectiveinkbooks.com
www.collectiveinkbooks.com
www.moon-books.net

For distributor details and how to order please visit the 'Ordering' section on our website.

ISBN: 978 1 78535 906 4
978 1 78535 907 1 (ebook)
Library of Congress Control Number: 2024940766

A CIP catalogue record for this book is available from the British Library.

Design: Lapiz Digital Services

UK: Printed and bound by CPI Group (UK) Ltd, Croydon, CR0 4YY
Printed in North America by CPI GPS partners

Contents

Foreword

It is the afternoon of the Spring Equinox, a damp and fresh March day in 1995. I have been invited to an Ostara celebration at the home of one of the staff at my residence hall at the University of North Texas, along with another of my friends. We're both relatively new to practicing Wicca, inspired by our readings of Starhawk and Scott Cunningham. We arrive at the cute little bungalow on a side street in our college town and, with some trepidation, knock on the front door. We are greeted by a group of women, most of them in the 30s and 40s, wearing bright tie dye, silver jewelry, and no shoes. We place our potluck contributions on the table in the tiny kitchen, then join the women in the dining room, where we are going to make masks of our faces with gauze strips covered in plaster. Nearby an array of paints, beads, rhinestones, feathers, and other fancy bits are laid out on a table covered in newspaper.

A woman I've never met before helps me coat my hairline with petroleum jelly, then begins gently smoothing the wet plaster strips over my face. I can't talk, because I have to keep my face still under the layers of mask as they're built. And so I listen. I listen to the laughter of the dozen or so women in the kitchen, in the living room setting up the altar. The sound is musical, magickal, and comforting all at the same time.

Our masks set; we leave them on the table to dry – each of them recognizable, unique, beautiful. We head to the living room, where the window is full of plants, the furniture has been pushed back a bit, and the coffee table has been transformed into an altar. I see all the Wiccan tools – athame and wand, chalice and bell – along with flowers and Goddess figures that I recognize from my recent art history class as "neolithic."

The priestess at the center creates the circle in the manner I've seen in Wiccan circles. We call the cardinal directions – North, East, South, and West – and the elements. The priestess invokes the Goddess, in her forms of Demeter, Persephone, Kore. I take a deep breath and wait for her to invoke the God, as we do in the Wiccan circles I've been to.

She doesn't. I feel my friend look at me with a question in her eyes. I raise my eyebrows and shake my head, equally confused. But as the priestess begins to speak, to tell the story of Demeter and Kore, of the Spring return, I find myself entranced. She leads us on a meditation where we see ourselves as the Kore, returning from our season in the underworld, where we have gone to heal and let go. She talks about the power of women, the power of the Goddess, the power of woman as Goddess. About finding and claiming our own power, rather than drawing power from something outside us.

And it occurs to me, that this is how it should be. That is what I was looking for when I started reading about witchcraft. That this is where I need to be. That this is what magick feels like.

I leave that celebration, many hours later, transformed.

I was 19 years old. And over 25 years later, I can say that my life has never been the same since that moment. That moment when I waited for the masculine form of God to be invoked, and that moment when I realized that my magick was complete without it. That moment when I looked around that living room and I saw the Goddess in the women around me, and they saw the Goddess in me.

I create this book in honor of those women, and in honor of the woman I was then and am becoming, and in honor of all the witches who have helped me grow in my magick, in my politics, and in my understanding these are not separate things.

Introduction

Witchcraft Has Always Been Political

> *"I don't know…I just don't like to mix politics with my religion."*

I can't count how many times I've heard this over the nearly three decades I've been practicing Witchcraft and moving in Witchy and Pagan communities. This type of conversation has definitely ramped up in the years I've been working on this book, four of which encompassed the Trump presidency in the United States, Brexit in the United Kingdom, the rise of White supremacist and nationalist movements around the globe, and so much else that has shaken the geopolitical sphere. The rise of a visible Witchcraft-based resistance to Donald Trump in the US, led largely by women and people of color, has amplified the discussions of the intersection of politics and religion within a lot of Witchy and Pagan communities in the United States as well. Even in the aftermath (and in the face of a potential resurgence) of Trump, conversations about witchcraft as activism are happening alongside conversations of more conventional Witchcraft topics.

My response is always the same:

> *You cannot extricate witchcraft from politics, because Witchcraft has always been political.*

Politics, as any anthropologist (including me) will tell you, is about far more than parties, elections, and voting systems. Politics at its heart is about *power* – who has it, who doesn't have it, how it's distributed, and who gets to have access to it.

Witchcraft, as any anthropologist (including me) will tell you, is about far more than potions, spells, and incantations. Witchcraft at its heart is about *power* – the power to influence reality, to exercise control over systems, to shape the world. While witchcraft looks different depending on cultural context, in every known society where witchcraft is found, it is about the ability to exercise power outside of the societally ordained power structure. Even in societies where witchcraft is considered to be universally evil, being suspected of being or known to be a witch conveys power on a person.

- To claim the label of Witch is to claim power.
- Witchcraft has always been, and will always be, political.
- For me personally, my Witchcraft is informed by feminist politics.

I am an anthropologist by training, and as such I always like to start by defining my terms. *Feminism* is the idea that there is no such thing as a lesser person, that all people deserve equality and dignity regardless of sex, gender, sexual orientation, race, class, or any other status. What differentiates it from other worldviews that also argue for equality is that it centers on gendered oppression, with special attention to the way gender intersects with other identities, as the root cause of many of society's ills.

I came up through what was euphemistically known as the "Women's Spirituality" movement of the 1980s and 1990s, and early on appreciated the clearly articulated link between the plight of the Earth and the plight of women. While my feminist politics have evolved quite a bit from those early days – more on that later in the pages that follow – from the beginning I found the idea of using Witchcraft to heal our planet, work changes in the global power structure, recover from the damage patriarchy does to women and girls, and create a most just and equitable world. It's a work in progress, a mission we might never fulfill, but one in which I still believe deeply.

The relationships I was encouraged to form with other women in the context of Women's Spirituality of Goddess Spirituality have been some of the most healing and empowering in my life. Learning to see the Sacred as embodied in a feminine form, quite a departure from my Church of Christ upbringing, was a paradigm shifter for me. To be able to see the Divine in the images of Goddesses from across time and across cultures, and then to begin to see that Sacredness in other women, was perhaps the biggest game changer for me in terms of my spirituality and my politics. And so was realizing that other women could see the Sacred in me, were encouraging me to find the Goddess in myself. Being encouraged to find the Sacred in myself *as a woman* and to see the sacredness in other women around me was a vital first step to healing the layers of personal and societal – even generational – trauma I carried, and I believe at my core that one of the ways we begin to recover from patriarchy is to find the Sacred within ourselves and do it without denying the Sacred within others.

It has been said that whenever women gather in circles, the world heals a little more. That healing, both personal and universal, is at the heart of my Craft. And I extend that healing to work to heal the planet and all that call Her home, to address injustice, to cast our spells and put our bodies on the line for justice and equity, to put our energies toward the better world we want. As we heal ourselves, we heal each other and the world around us – and that is an amazing claiming of power.

If what I've written above intrigues you, appeals to you, or gives you *feelings*, then this book is for you. As I complete this manuscript in the spring and summer of 2024, global forces are at work that are filling many of us with worry, fear, and a sense of powerlessness. At the same time, we are seeing a resurgence in the interest in and the practice of witchcraft in various forms, of witchcraft as a form of resistance to the gathering clouds of political and climate catastrophe that loom on the horizon. The pages that follow are not intended to be prescriptive, to lay out a definitive or end-all and be-all of practice Feminist Witchcraft. Instead, they are an invitation for you to explore ways to (re) politicize your witchcraft practice, to form circles of support and power and resistance, and to step into your power.

Let's get started. Time is of the essence.

Chapter 1
Foundations

Why Feminism? Why Witchcraft? Why Feminist Witchcraft?

If you've picked up this book, it's likely you've read more than one introduction to Wicca or other forms of Witchcraft, and you're likely asking yourself what makes Feminist Witchcraft different from all of those you've read about before. In truth, there are many overlaps with the Feminist Witchcraft I practice and other forms of Witchcraft and Contemporary Pagan spirituality and magickal[1] practice. But there are also a few things that set it apart, and it is these specific characteristics that drew me to the practice of Feminist Witchcraft rather than just the eclectic Wicca that is far more common in my Pagan and magickal community. I jokingly say that I came for the transcendence and stayed for the politics, but there's more than a grain of truth in that jest. I was drawn to Feminist Witchcraft because it made explicit the connection between power and resistance, between transformation in the spiritual world and social change in the physical world, and between the personal and the collective. It was the first overtly political form of spiritual practice I'd encountered – or at least the first one that centered politics that mirrored my own. While I believe that all Witchcraft is at its heart political, choosing to practice a Craft that is intrinsically rooted in feminist politics is what feels most authentic for me.

A Quick Note on Terminology

Throughout this book, there are several terms I will use somewhat interchangeably for the type of Witchcraft I am talking about. I will refer to it variously as Feminist Witchcraft, Feminist Craft, or (sometimes, rarely) Goddess Craft. You will also encounter the terms Feminist Spirituality, Women's Spirituality, and Goddess Spirituality as you make your way through these chapters, particularly when I discuss historical foundations of Feminist Witchcraft in the United States and other areas of the West. Each of these terms has its own subtle shades of meaning, and I tend to move back and forth among them. The exception is Women's Spirituality, which I only use when discussing the historical underpinnings of Feminist Craft, because I do not believe that the practice of Feminist Witchcraft needs to be limited to cisgender[2] women alone – one of the places I differ strongly with the founders of the Feminist Witchcraft movement in the US, as we will explore later.

Throughout this book, I will use the term *women* to refer to both cisgender and transgender women – trans women are always included when I speak about women. In cases where the distinction matters, as in discussions of exclusion of trans women or the founding mothers of Feminist Craft limiting their definition of womanhood to cisgender women, I will use more precise language or will add footnotes for clarification. I also at times use the term "non-men" to refer to people who are not women but who are also not men – nonbinary people, genderfluid people, and agender people, among others. This language is imperfect but is at the time of this writing the best solution I can come up with to work around the binary nature of English terms for gender.

The Dreaded F Word

So let's get the dreaded F-word out of the way, shall we? A full explanation of everything feminism is (and isn't) would require this book to be twice as long, and even then it would probably be incomplete. For our purposes here, I'll distill feminism as I understand and practice it down a bit, and I also encourage those of you who want a more in-depth discussion to explore the resources at the end of this book.

Simply put, feminism as I understand and practice it is a social movement for equality, equity, and justice for all people regardless of gender, sexual orientation, race, ethnicity, class, dis/ability, or other social status. Feminism is the idea that there is no such thing as a lesser person, that all people deserve equality, equity, justice, and dignity. I know what some of you are thinking: Why not call it *humanism* or *equalism*? Well, *humanism* already applies to another social movement – one in which people believe that humans do not need gods or divine beings to guide them or give them meaning. (Many humanist beliefs are indeed feminist and otherwise pro-equality, but the word has other important meanings as well.) *Equalism* is a term that's often used by people who actually want to deny that inequality exists or to assert that all people share the same level of oppression, and thus specific movements for gender, racial, disability, or queer justice are no longer needed. Neither is satisfactory to me. I prefer the word (and the concept) of feminism because it foregrounds gender as an axis of oppression, and for me – a white, bisexual, cisgender, enabled[3] woman – it is the axes of gender and sexual orientation that have been the primary sites of social oppression and marginalization for me. It is meaningful to me to look at the move for social equality through gender as a primary (though not sole) lens.

Why Witchcraft?

Witchcraft as I practice it is embedded within a religious framework but is not synonymous with any particular religious system. While Wicca is perhaps the form of Witchcraft most Americans are familiar with, and my own practice shares some overlap with Wiccan structure, the two are not one in the same. Witchcraft for me is, following Starhawk,[4] the art of changing consciousness at will to effect change in the real world. It can be practiced alongside any theology or lack of theology, within any religious system or without any religious system at all. I make the distinction in this book between *feminist witchcraft* (any type of witchcraft practiced with a feminist ethos) and *Feminist Witchcraft* (Earth-centered, Goddess-centered witchcraft which draws on the Western feminist, Women's Spirituality, and Goddess movements of the late 20th century and which has considerable overlap with the larger Contemporary Pagan movement in the West).

My own Feminist Witchcraft is deeply embedded in Goddess and Earth-centered spirituality, which inform both my practice and my politics. When I talk about Witchcraft in this book, I am talking about this flexible and adaptable system of working with energies and natural elements to create impactful and real world change.

Witchcraft seems to me particularly well suited to a feminist ethos, though it is far from the only religion or spirituality that can be practiced from a feminist standpoint. The appeal of witchcraft for me has always lay in its insistence that we reclaim our own personal power and our right to function as agents in the world. Women in particular are often encouraged to live our life as subjects – beings to be acted upon, rather than beings who act. Witchcraft is the ability to act in the world and to make one's will manifest. Witchcraft also does not require that we go through a hierarchy to access our power – everything we need already exists within us. We may need to learn techniques and tools, but the raw power to affect change exists within us, is inherent to our human existence.

Witchcraft has also historically been a tool of the marginalized and oppressed, a tool people have used to take back power from institutions and social structures that would deny them access to formal avenues of power and agency.[5] This means it has been a tool of women, of other non-men, of queer folks, of indigenous people in the face of colonialism, and of people of color in white supremacist societies. The image of the witch has been used as a form of social control across history and around the world, especially weaponized against those who resist social norms or otherwise do not conform to societal expectations. Witchcraft is, fundamentally, about resistance, and as such is a tool for both collective and personal liberation.

I believe that Witchcraft is a powerful tool for personal, collective, and societal healing. In America and in much of the Western world, we are encouraged to use our Craft as part of our personal healing journeys, and indeed this is an important piece of what the practice of Witchcraft does in our lives. However, I think we miss the point if we stop at our own personal healing and growth. We are all part of the interconnected web of life, to borrow from Starhawk's metaphor, and as such we need to see our own healing and liberation as bound up with that of all other humans, all other creatures, and indeed the planet herself.

Why Feminist Witchcraft?

So what makes any given form of witchcraft feminist – or not feminist? Some social scientists and practitioners argue that all witchcraft that is practiced under the Pagan umbrella (and more specifically under the Wiccan umbrella) is by default feminist, because women hold positions of leadership and because the Feminine Divine is venerated alongside the Masculine Divine. The presence of a Goddess alone, they argue, is enough to qualify Wicca and other Pagan religions that involve the practice of witchcraft as feminist. I counter argue that there are societies throughout the world that venerate goddesses but that do not entail equality of even high quality of life for women. Likewise, women may rise to leadership in religious movements that go on to enact practices and advocate for social policies that oppress women and other groups of marginalized people. While religions such as Wicca may have some tenets that espouse feminist or proto-feminist ideals, the type of feminist witchcraft I practice and advocate for is a bit different, a bit more explicitly political.

The Feminist Witchcraft I practice has a few basic features and core assertions/assumptions:

- It is important for people to venerate a Divine that looks like them; this is an inalienable human right. For women, this often means the veneration of a Goddess or Feminine Divine.
- Gender inequality is a primary force in the lives of women and other non-men. It is not the only force, but it is a major one. We have the right to use all the tools at our disposal to fight that.
- The figure of the witch has been used to oppress and harm women and other marginalized people throughout history. Reclaiming the image of the witch and the power it entails is a major step toward reclaiming our own power and fighting oppression.
- Witchcraft is a tool for personal healing, spiritual growth, and political resistance. It has been so historically and can and should be used for these ends now.
- Witchcraft is a tool for collective liberation and healing. It has been so historically and should be used for these ends now.

With these foundations established, we can now move into the meat – or the tofu, if you prefer – of our venture into Feminist Craft. As we move forward through the next chapters, I invite readers whose practice may not share the same Contemporary Pagan flavor as my own to incorporate whatever aspects of this book and the practice I describe into their own Craft – as well as to leave the portions that don't work for them. One of the major appeals about Witchcraft as a system for me is its innate adaptability, flexibility, and openness to innovation. Each practitioner brings to the practice their own backstory, identities, experiences, and understandings of the world. To incorporate these into your Witchcraft practice is perhaps the greatest act of magick of all.

Chapter 2

The Goddess

In the title of her foundational text on Wicca, *The Spiral Dance*, Starhawk called Witchcraft "the religion of the Great Goddess." Contemporary Pagan Witchcraft, of which Wicca is probably the most well-known branch, is often called "Goddess religion" or "the religion of the Goddess" as well. Claims of ancient links between Witchcraft and Goddess worship throughout Prehistoric Western Europe are shaky at best and specious at worst, but Contemporary Paganism and Witchcraft have been undeniably Goddess-centered since their emergence in the 19th and 20th centuries. When one first encounters most iterations of Contemporary Paganism, the Goddess (whether She is accompanied by a God or not) is often the most striking feature.

Feminist Witchcraft is at its heart Goddess-centered, though what that means can vary depending on the Witch in question. The centrality of the Goddess (sometimes simply referred to as "Goddess" without the definite article), most often to the exclusion of any God or Masculine Divine, is perhaps *the* defining feature that differentiates Feminist Witchcraft from Wicca or other forms of Contemporary Witchcraft. The political reasons for a primary or sole focus on the Goddess in Feminist Witchcraft will be discussed in a bit more depth later, but for now, we'll take a closer look at the question of who the Goddess *is*.

Who Is the Goddess?

It's something of an axiom that if you bring 13 Witches together and ask them who the Goddess is, you'll get 14 different answers. Some people will respond by discussing specific, distinct Goddesses from a given pantheon or pantheons. Others will speak about a universal Divine Feminine force that is understood through the images of different Goddesses in different places and times, who are all aspects of that One Feminine Divine. Still others might evoke a framework familiar to Wiccans, where the Goddess is one half of a duality completed by the God. Others might speak of archetypes, or symbolic personification of the Universal Life Force. And still others may speak of the Goddess as the embodiment of the Feminine Principle in the Universe.

And they're all right.

Because of its roots in the Women's Spirituality movement, and because a central tenet of that movement was the reclamation of a Feminine Face of God,[6] Feminist Witchcraft is by its nature Goddess-centered. The thealogy[7] that underpins Feminist Witchcraft it is not prescriptive, but is instead personal, political, and experiential. While Goddess thealogians like Carol P. Christ and Rosemary Reuther (among many others) have written extensively on Goddess-based frameworks and worldviews, none of these are taken as canon or (forgiving the pun) gospel truth. Rather, they are presented as potential models for understanding a Goddess worldview, especially for those who want to move beyond Abrahamic frameworks and the patriarchal social institutions underpinned by them. In order to imagine a new way of relating to ourselves and the planet Herself, these writers argued, we must relate to Divinity differently. For some Feminist Witches, like myself, this means that the Masculine Divine as symbolized by a male God is not part of their practice. Most of the early writers on Feminist Witchcraft craft rituals around the Goddess alone, rather than the more familiar God-Goddess dyad found in much of Wicca. Some Feminist Craft traditions do recognize a God or male deity but tend to place him somewhat lower in status than the Goddess herself. Personally I find that that does little but recreate the same sexist dynamic which erased and debased Goddess, and I choose not to work with Divinity in this way.

So, do you need to "believe" in the Goddess in order to practice Feminist Craft? Well, no. To paraphrase Starhawk, Witches don't believe in the Goddess – we experience Her. But in a broader sense, there is no need to believe in a Divinity or Higher Power if you want to practice Feminist Craft. The engagement with power, and particularly the power of Nature, is to me more fundamental than any belief in a discreet or universal Goddess, and I believe that power can be found within ourselves and within circles of other practitioners. I have practiced alongside many atheist and humanist Feminist Witches who found their power not in the idea of a Goddess but instead through observing Nature itself and finding awe and sacredness there, and in finding the sacred and the powerful in themselves and other humans.

Belief in the Goddess or any sort of Divine is not required to practice Feminist Witchcraft, and I would argue that even those of us who do assert the existence of the Goddess in one form or another do not "believe" in her in the sense that "belief in God" is so often used in Western culture. Rather, I contend that we *experience* Goddess through interactions with Nature, through participating in ritual, through coming to know and value ourselves. If, as Starhawk has said, witches are people who are paying attention, then we come to know the Goddess through paying attention to the everyday moments of sacredness that permeate our lives. In fact, the ability – even the necessity – of humans to directly experience Divinity and to find the Divine in ourselves is a direct outgrowth of the politics that underlie the emergence of Feminist Witchcraft in the first place.

Ultimately, however, the way any individual practitioner of Feminist Craft understands the Goddess is intensely personal, and it may be fluid and shift over time. (My own personal thealogy has shifted from a monist "Universal Life Force with many manifestations" to a more humanist perspective over my three decades of practice.) While some may find this fluidity and squishiness frustrating, others (including myself) find freedom in getting to determine what relationship, if any, we engage in with Divinity.

A Quick Primer on Feminist Theology

One of the driving forces behind the Women's Spirituality movement that gave rise to Feminist Witchcraft as I practice it was the desire to reclaim the Feminine Divine. The Second Wave Feminism of the 1970s was deeply critical of the patriarchal nature of Western religion, and of Christianity in particular, and saw the exclusive focus on the Masculine Divine as underpinning much gender inequality in the West. Feminist theologian Mary Daly[8] infamously intoned, "When God is male, the male is God," in her 1973 speech "Beyond God the Father," and other early writers in the Women's Spirituality and Goddess movement also pointed to the lack of Feminine Divine in Abrahamic faiths as oppressive to women. While not all the writers in the Women's Spirituality movement advocated placing a Goddess or Feminine Divine at the center of religion as a way to address these problems, a number of them did. Carol P. Christ's 1978 essay "Why Women Need the Goddess" articulated the ways in which the loss of access to the Feminine Divine harmed women and created a culture in which women are systematically devalued. This essay, first delivered as a keynote speech, effectively kicked off the modern Goddess movement in the US, which in turns underlies much of Feminist Witchcraft as it is practiced today. Christ's central argument, and one that is common throughout much of early Feminist Spirituality and Feminist Witchcraft writing, is that by making God solely male in Western thought, society has deprived women of the ability to see themselves as divine and sacred – and has by extension allowed for the denigration of women on a societal level. Reclaiming the Goddess/Feminine Divine allows women to reclaim their own sacredness, which is key to addressing gender-based oppression and the social and personal ills that flow from it.

Why Center the Goddess?

So why center the Goddess? Doesn't that just replicate the same erasure that Feminist Witches are critiquing, but with the genders flipped? Don't we need both Goddess and God to have a balanced view of Divinity?

Certainly, some Witches do feel that it's necessary to work with both a God and a Goddess in order to balance what they term masculine and feminine energies. Within Feminist Craft as I practice it, however, is the idea that we can balance these seemingly polar energies without conflating them with human ideas of gender. Although I recognize the importance and the historical use of the terms "masculine" and "feminine" to denote two different types of energies we can work with in spiritual practice, I increasingly have engaged in feminist critique of these terminologies as bioessentialist and reductive, and ultimately harmful to humans of all genders (of which there are more than two). I find myself drawn to the terms ``projective" and "magnetic" (borrowed from my good friend, queer astrologist Colin Bedell) rather than the customary gendered binary.

Centering the Goddess is also important in Feminist Craft because by centering Her, we also center the human women who are Her embodiment on Earth.[9] The earliest writers in the Goddess Movement drew a direct line from the treatment of the Earth herself to the treatment of human women, and made explicit that centering the Earth (as embodied in the Goddess) and demanding that environmental exploitation be addressed and stopped was part and parcel of the liberation of women and the ending of gender-based violence – two of feminism's central goals. By seeing the parallels between the degradation of the Earth and the degradation and exploitation of human women, these thealogians created a system in which the Goddess was not just reclaimed in the context of white, masculine, heteropatriarchy (or what Rosemary Radford termed *Kyriarchy*, a specific kind of patriarchy where only certain men and the people adjacent to them hold power and reap society's benefits), but called for the fundamental rethinking of the ways in which society is organized.

Some of the earliest writers on Goddess spirituality and Feminist Witchcraft felt that centering the Goddess was a return to a pre-patriarchal, more egalitarian way of being. These authors drew heavily on the archaeological work of Marija Gimbutas and Merlin Stone, among others, and these writings about the prehistoric matriarchy have come to form a kind of sacred history for the Feminist Witchcraft and Goddess movements. These works form a body of mythopoetics that still informs the types of rituals, symbols, and creative works that permeate many Feminist Witchcraft spaces, including the images of the Goddess Herself, often depicted in a Paleolithic or Neolithic style akin to the Venus of Willendorf or other so-called "Venus" figures. As an anthropologist and gender scholar myself I find the arguments for some sort of peaceful, feminist, Goddess-centered matriarchal prehistory to be lacking in rigor and instead to represent a kind of fanciful reimagining of human history, in an attempt to justify Goddess religion as somehow older and thus more valid than Christianity. I also tend to agree with sociologist Cynthia Eller when she writes that building a religion with an "invented past" does not really give women a future to aspire to.[10] Ultimately I am less concerned with what humans may or may not have done in prehistory and more concerned with the new ways of relating to each other, to the planet, and to the Divine that we can create *now*.

That said, I recognize that these sacred mythopoetics were doing important work in the founding of Feminist Witchcraft, in encouraging people to think beyond the seemingly-inescapable patriarchal and capitalist systems in which we in the West are embedded. The need to create a different world than the one in which we are currently living, with its social inequalities and injustices, its climate degradation, and its wars and conflicts was a central project of Second Wave feminism, particularly the Radical Feminism that gave rise to Goddess Spirituality and Feminist Witchcraft. Providing another vision of how we might live with each other, these writings inspired generations of Feminist Witches to experiment with different forms of leadership, community building, relationship structures, and more. For that reason, I believe that such early texts are important to read and appreciate, even while we remain able to see their flaws and critique them.

A common central theme within the sacred mythopoetics of Goddess Spirituality and Feminist Witchcraft, and one that I find immensely valuable, is the focus on the body as a site of sacredness. I have said that belief in Goddess is not a requirement to practice Feminist Witchcraft, and that is largely because Witchcraft as a whole, and Feminist Witchcraft in particular, is an experiential religion. We are encouraged to experience Goddess and the Sacred through the body as well as the mind.

The Goddess in the Body: Feminist Witchcraft as Embodied Practice

Beyond even the explicit reclaiming of a Feminine Divine, what was and remains most attractive to me about Goddess Spirituality, and thus about Feminist Witchcraft, is that it is fundamentally an embodied practice. It is not something I "believe" with my brain. It is something I experience through my body, through every one of my senses, and through my relationships. The Goddess is not a theoretical or abstract concept for me – She moves freely through my life in tangible, observable ways, and arguably She moves through me because She *is* me and I am Her. The encouragement I found in Feminist

Witchcraft to celebrate my body, honor my body, and challenge the cultural messages I had received about the sinfulness of the body in general, and of the bodies of women and girls in particular, ran so counter to the body-denying and body-denigrating Christianity in which I was raised, and I found and continue to find it profoundly healing. That I could come to know Divinity – and more importantly, to find Divinity in myself – through experiencing the world through my very earthly body was a revelation.

Learning to see my body as an instrument of the Divine and a vehicle for magick remains the most precious gift Feminist Witchcraft has given me. Witchcraft cross culturally is profoundly embodied – it involves dancing, singing, intense experiences of sensory input or deprivation, eating and drinking, and sharing touch with other humans. I have appreciated the ways in which I *feel* Witchcraft in my body when I participate in rituals, whether they be Feminist Witchcraft or more mainstream Wiccan circles. But Feminist Witchcraft takes this one step further for me, by making this embodiment and reclaiming of the body explicitly political. Feminist Witchcraft and Goddess Spirituality encourage me to see my body as sacred not simply because it was a human body, but because it was a *woman's body*[11], in a society that has consistently denigrated, commodified, and abused the bodies of women and girls (and other non-men). It was the antidote to the poisonous message that the bodies of women are the site of original sin, of pollution. As someone who had been exposed to toxic messages about my body as somehow less than, with its menstrual cycles and potential to give birth and all the rest, and who had been subjected to abuse and trauma because of the body I inhabit, hearing alternative messaging that these things were not only sources of sin or pollution but were in fact sites of sacredness was profoundly healing.

Before I go further, I want to take a moment to acknowledge that much of the early writing on Goddess Spirituality and

Feminist Witchcraft focused on the idea of "women's bodies" or "female bodies" in a way I now know to be cis-centric and cis-normative.[12] I did not recognize these at the time because my own education on gender, as well as the dominant cultural conversation about gender at the time, was itself shaped by ideas of binary gender, biological essentialism, and cisnormativity. As my own education and the cultural conversation have expanded to include different understandings of gender, I have begun critiquing these early writings (and writings that reinforce them), engaged in a great deal of soul-searching about them, and adjusted my own practice and language to be inclusive of trans woman, nonbinary people, and others who might have been excluded by Feminist Craft, whether explicitly or implicitly. I have also had to make peace with the fact that I found much of the writing about the sacredness of the "female" body healing and revolutionary, and that I still find deep meaning in many of the practices and works of art I was exposed to, even as I recognize that they might have the opposite impact on others who are exposed to them. This is an ongoing process, always, and I am forever learning more about it.

I also want to acknowledge that many of the founders of Feminist Witchcraft at the time and still today hold views about what a "woman's body" is that are rooted in biological essentialism – simply put, that to be a woman one must possess a vulva, vagina, uterus, and ovaries, and that people who possess these body parts are inherently women. These ideas about the body have been used to exclude, sometimes explicitly and violently, trans women and nonbinary people from Feminist Witchcraft spaces and (somewhat paradoxically) to erase trans men in those same spaces by treating them as butch women. I do want to state unequivocally that when I talk about "women's bodies" in the context of Feminist Witchcraft, I am not limiting it to the bodies of cisgender women. Nor do I consider bodies that possess uterus, ovaries, etc. to be inherently "women's" bodies. I believe there is value and healing to be found in celebrating and reclaiming the aspects of the body that have been stigmatized. For cisgender women like myself, this can mean honoring menstruation, childbirth, and menopause as sacred and reflections of Goddess. Nonbinary people who menstruate or give birth may also find power in honoring these bodily processes, and should be encouraged to celebrate them in ways that feel good. Trans women's bodies are often stigmatized in different – but no less damaging – ways than cis women's bodies, and I fully believe it is important for trans women to honor, reclaim, and celebrate their bodies as reflection of the Goddess, if that is something that would be healing and meaningful to the person in question.

Finally, I hope it is clear from what I've just said that I support the inclusion of trans women and nonbinary folks in Feminist Spirituality and Feminist Witchcraft spaces such as open rituals, festivals and gatherings, study groups, and retreats. There still exist spaces like this that explicitly exclude anyone who is not a cisgender woman by limiting them to "women born women only." While the needle has moved considerably in the direction of trans inclusion in the last decade, the anti-trans backlash of the 2020s and the weaponized language of "protecting women's spaces" that has accompanied it has renewed calls for trans exclusion in some Feminist Spirituality and Feminist Witchcraft spaces. I wholeheartedly reject trans exclusion in my spiritual spaces, and I do not attend or endorse events that have exclusionary policies. I encourage my readers to also advocate for Feminist Witchcraft spaces that include transgender women and nonbinary folks who feel called to them.

Goddess Spirituality as Relationship

Goddess Spirituality is fundamentally relational. By this I mean, those of us who choose to work with the Goddess in our Feminist Witchcraft build a relationship with Her, and that relationship is quite different than what one might find in the monotheistic traditions of the West, or even in the polytheistic traditions within Contemporary Paganism writ large.

You will notice that I have thus far avoided the term "Goddess Worship" to describe what I do in my Craft, and this is entirely intentional. The term *worship* is loaded with a sense of power-over for me, with an image of a relationship in which one party holds the power and the other party is the supplicant. I have never found power in this type of relationship with Deity, and in fact this type of power relationship was one of the things I sought to escape about the particular variety of Christianity in which I was raised. I was seeking something far more egalitarian, and found it in the Feminist Witchcraft circles I encountered early in my practice. Leadership among the women in those spaces was egalitarian, and we were encouraged to create an egalitarian, adult to adult (rather than child to parent) relationship with Goddess as well. After all, we were all Goddess embodied, right? Why wouldn't we approach Her as though we were equals, created equally Divine?

I can hear the brakes being pumped right now out there, so stick with me for a moment. Westerners are definitely not taught to approach Deity this way, and may in fact be told that to consider one's self a manifestation of the Divine or on equal footing with the Divine to be an act of hubris, the sin of pride. But hear me out. The Goddess Spirituality at the heart of Feminist Craft as I practice it is a system in which the notion of sin is absent, and in which we are encouraged to claim our own power. Recognizing our inherent Divinity is a path to reclaiming that power. And part of that is learning to take charge of a situation using the tools at our disposal – and that certainly includes witchcraft and all the spiritual technologies that fall under that name, which we will discuss in a later chapter. Feminist Witches work *with* the Goddess, and certainly learn to draw Her power into ourselves and our workings, but we do not, to garble an old cliche, "let go and let Goddess." Willful abdication of power is not part of the system in which Feminist Witchcraft works.

But wait, didn't you just say a few paragraphs up that there is no one way to understand Goddess within Feminist Craft? Yep, sure did. And I stand by that. The relational, egalitarian approach I describe above is what works for me, and what I have seen as a common thread in Feminist Witchcraft circles over nearly three decades of practice. However, I also recognize that an individual Feminist Witch might come to a different understanding of their relationship to Goddess, and that's not for me to gatekeep. I have performed powerful acts of feminist, justice-centered magick with people who were hard polytheists, reverent agnostics, and atheists, among others. What was important in those workings was that our Craft was performed from a feminist and justice-centered standpoint. Everything else is between a Witch and their Goddess (or lack of Goddess).

For Feminist Witches of a theist bent, there are many different ways one might choose to work with Goddess. You may find your relationship to Goddess changing over your lifetime as well. I was a pretty hard theist when I first encountered Feminist Craft, and spent years working with specific Goddesses from different pantheons. Over time, my relationship with Goddess has evolved to be a more humanist one, though I find power in Goddess images and sacred stories from around the world and across time. If all that seems as clear as mud, you're not alone. We're not very well equipped in Western culture to talk about Divinity without falling back on the tropes inherent in the Abrahamic faiths – and particularly Christianity – that so many of us are raised with and which still underpin so much of our language and society. I will, however, try. Here is a (non-exhaustive) list of the ways a Feminist Witch might find themselves relating to Goddess in their practice.

You might find yourself working very directly with one Goddess or several from a specific pantheon. Many of the Feminist Witches I have known have worked with Diana (so much so that Dianic Witchcraft is a specific path of Feminist Witchcraft). Others may choose to work with Hecate, or the Morrighan. In this type of practice, these Goddesses are concrete beings with personalities and presences of their own – Diana is not interchangeable with another moon Goddess, for example. There's a lot of discussion among theist folks about whether or not one should work with Goddesses from different pantheons, or whether this is disrespectful. There's also a whole other discussion about whether one should work with Goddesses from pantheons outside one's own heritage. These are complicated and personal issues, in my view, and I encourage people to read, research, and listen to their own spirit and to the voice of Goddess herself in making these choices. Because this is not my personal approach to working with Goddess, I do not have much guidance, but you will find much writing out there in the larger Pagan and Witchcraft spheres if you want to explore this type of relationship with the Divine.

Another approach to working with Goddess – perhaps the most common I have seen in US Feminist Witchcraft spaces – is to invoke or use the images of various Goddesses from different pantheons. In this approach, these individual Goddesses are seen as facets or faces of the larger Feminine Divine – you'll see the term "She of 10,000 Faces" used to describe Goddess in many writings and works of art. The myriad Goddesses from around the world and across time are seen as manifestations of Goddess, rather than as distinct beings. Calling forth a specific aspect of the Goddess, under the name or names of specific Goddesses, brings that energy to your working. So a circle asking for healing might invoke Sulis, while a rite of passage might invoke Inanna and Persephone. Myths and sacred stories are seen as maps for our human experience, and the Goddesses that inhabit those stories are our guides. And while they each have their own faces and stories, they are all aspects of Goddess as a whole. (I have written about this approach, called monism, in *Naming the Goddess*).

You might choose to go even more abstract and see Goddess as an extended metaphor for life itself, and to find inspiration in sacred stories and mythic cycles while not actually invoking or using the images of any culturally specific Goddess. Instead you might find power in Neolithic inspired sculptures or other images of women or that whisper "Goddess" to you. You might believe in an actual Divine Feminine Higher Being, or may just find the metaphor of Goddess useful for you without believing in a personal Divine at all. This approach is much about working with symbols and energy, which are themselves powerful, rather than drawing on an external being or source of power. My own more humanist approach fits in here. I do not believe that humans need Divinity at all to be good, but I recognize the power in sacred images and stories, and I find it incredibly important to include feminine images in the canon.

If all this feels like a whole lot of abstract thought – and you're not the kind of person who's ever even idly entertained going to divinity school – don't despair. While an understanding of the thealogy underpinning Feminist Witchcraft is useful, especially as you navigate your own relationship with Goddess, the theological questions aren't necessarily the point. They're a jumping off place to the aspects of Feminist Witchcraft which are arguably the most powerful – the politics and the practice.

Chapter 3

The Witch

Why choose Witchcraft as the cornerstone of a feminist religious practice? There are a lot of reasons, and there has been a great deal of writing on the topic, but one major reason is that the Witch herself has been a significant symbol of power, and particularly the power held by women, throughout history and across cultures. Even in cultures in which Witches are stigmatized and have been (and still are) persecuted, the power of the Witch has never been denied. As I discussed earlier, Witchcraft has always been about the claiming and exercise of power. And while people of diverse genders have always been, still are, and will always be Witches and capable of powerful Craft, the power of the Witch has been most often associated with women (and to some degree with anyone of a gender other than man).

Witchcraft accusations cross-culturally have been a way of enforcing social norms, especially gender norms, and of punishing those who step outside those norms. Who else to choose as a folk hero and sacred symbol than the woman who pushes social boundaries and exercises her own power and terrifies the existing social order in the process?

Feminist reclamations of the *Witch* have stressed the ways in which knowledge typically associated with women (and other marginalized genders, but predominantly women given the persistence of the gender binary in the West and regions that have been subject to Western colonialism) have been lumped under the label of Witchcraft – herbal healing, contraception, abortion, birth, preparation of the dead, even knowledge of gardening and animals and Nature generally. A return to a more holistic way of living was one of the major features of the

Second Wave of feminism that gave rise to Feminist Witchcraft in the US, and so it is unsurprising that in exploring these bodies of knowledge, the image of the Witch re-emerged.

Starhawk has written that reclaiming the image and the word Witch is key to reclaiming our own power. It is a word that has been, and in many regions of the world still is, used to hurt people – most of them women, LGBTQAI+, or otherwise non-gender-normative people – who step outside the bounds of what is considered proper and appropriate for them. Recognizing *Witch* as a word imbued with power and taking it as a mantle for oneself can be key in shifting our view of power, including our own agency.

And Witchcraft, as we typically frame it in Western Contemporary Pagan circles and in Feminist Witchcraft in particular, is all about agency. Witchcraft is something we *do*, most often in response to a need or desire to effect change in some area of our world. Witchcraft is our way of asserting that we have some control or influence over our own lives, of taking a situation in hand and using the available resources to influence an outcome. While Witchcraft should never be the *only* tool brought to bear on a situation, it is one of the many technologies we have available and can be an incredible source of empowerment. And for this reason, I (along with other writers and practitioners) think that Witchcraft and Feminism make an ideal pairing – they are both concerned with bringing about change, both concerned with marginalized and disempowered people taking back their power from a system that would deny them. While Witchcraft might not be the *only* spiritual system that supports and is supported by feminist values, the two do seem natural (forgiving the pun) sisters.

Finally, Witchcraft is well suited to an explicitly political spiritual practice (and an explicitly *feminist* political spiritual practice) because, as I discussed in the Foreword, Witchcraft has historically been, and remains, one of the tools used by the marginalized and oppressed to fight back against systems of oppression. While I don't want to draw too close a comparison between, say, the middle class White women in my Goddess circles and people who have borne up under systems such as slavery or repressive regimes around the world, I do think it is useful to see the ways in which oppressed groups have some common cause and thus might turn to Witchcraft and other similar sacred technologies to exercise agency and combat oppression. Certainly the rise in interest in Witchcraft, and particularly Witchcraft directed at social justice and political aims, during the presidency of Donald Trump speaks to the ways in which even today people who find themselves up against a repressive system will reach for Witchcraft as a tool – or a weapon.

Embracing the Witch

Unlike more traditional Witchcraft traditions such as Wicca, there is no set hierarchy within Feminist Witchcraft. There is no lengthy learning process, and no formal initiation unless the individual Witch desires such a ceremony to mark the rite of passage of claiming the name of Witch. We do not "become" Feminist Witches – we embrace the fact that we *already are Witches at our core*. We take the time to learn the skills and Craft of Witchcraft, but all the essential tools we need are already held within us. A common maxim in early Feminist Witchcraft writings is that "every woman is a Witch." I believe this to be true, and I believe that people who are not women can and do have a Witch inside them waiting to be embraced.

How do we embrace the Witch within? I've always liked the statement from Second Wave Feminist activist group WITCH (Women's International Conspiracy from Hell) that encouraged women to say "I am a Witch" three times before a mirror, and then really think about what that meant. While WITCH in its original form was a performance art group and not a Witchcraft group per se, I find their use of the image of the Witch as symbolic of our inherent power to shape the world power and evocative. Consider starting your Feminist Witchcraft journey by standing before the mirror and speaking the words "I am a Witch" and reflecting on how you feel!

A key aspect of embracing the Witch within and beginning a journey into Feminist Witchcraft is taking the time to see the sacred in the everyday, the magickal in the small moments. It may be tempting to assume that you need to give yourself a crash course in feminist politics and occult science to embark on this path. And while continuing to read and raise your awareness of both those things, as well as paying attention to the very real issues at work in the world around you, will be vital to using your Craft towards greater justice, in a very real way the first steps into Feminist Witchcraft are very small. A well-worn maxim of feminism is that the personal is political. When we begin to embrace our own power and to foster our own growth, it's not just personal healing – it's a political act of seizing our power back from kyriarchy, from the forces that would tell us that we are not powerful beings. And while simply doing this work on the personal level won't necessarily change the world or end injustice, it does equip us to imagine a different world, a more just world, and to relate to each other and to ourselves in a justice- and love-centered way that *does* allow us to work for wider societal change.

One of my first teachers in Feminist Craft told me "Your first year in the Craft is all about facing your shit." While it might not be an elegant statement, and probably won't show up on any Instagram posts anytime soon, this might be one of the truest things anyone has ever said to me about Witchcraft. Witchcraft is above all a tool for healing – for healing others, for healing the Earth Herself, and for healing ourselves from the damage done to us on macro and micro scales. No one escapes a patriarchy or a kyriarchy unscathed, and women and other people who are not men bear much of the brunt of this systemic violence. And that's before we even begin to touch all the traumas and injuries that happen to us within our families, our relationships, and our personal journeys through this life. I do not believe anyone has to be "perfectly healed" or "entirely whole" to practice Witchcraft – if this were true, there would be vanishing few Witches on the planet. Rather, I believe that as we enter into Witchcraft, and especially politically centered Witchcraft, we have a duty to recognize the damage that has been done to us, and the damage we have inflicted on others and on the planet, and take steps towards healing those things. Witchcraft is just one technology we can use to heal the wounds of patriarchy, kyriarchy, capitalism, and all the myriad sources of injury we encounter, and it should not be the only one – I am a strong advocate of therapy and other mental healthcare (and for it being accessible to all), for education, for medical and complementary healthcare, and for any other tool that we can use to bring ourselves to more balance and wholeness. I do believe, however, that Witchcraft (and perhaps spirituality more generally, but most definitely Witchcraft) allows us to face, name, and heal things that the other technologies available to us cannot touch. The act of taking one's power back is in and of itself a path to healing, to wholeness, and authenticity.

Feminist Witchcraft is a sacred technology that equips us to take our power back. In the next chapters, we'll move from theory to practice and examine specific tools and techniques we can use in that reclamation.

Chapter 4

Healing from Patriarchy and Kyriarchy

Like many of the women who found Witchcraft via the Women's Spirituality movement of the 1970s-1990s, I came to embrace the Witch archetype as part of healing from patriarchy. As a young woman who was raised with one foot in fairly conservative Protestant Christianity, under capitalism, and in the midst of the backlash to the gains of Second Wave feminism in the United States, my late teens and early twenties were filled with uncomfortable realizations of the ways in which patriarchal religion, capitalism, and social structures had left me with deep wounds, exposed me to various type of violence, and undermined my sense of self. It was in searching for an alternative to the religious systems I had always known that I eventually wandered into my first women's circles and experienced Witchcraft firsthand.

Feminist Witchcraft is explicitly about healing from the damage of patriarchy and kyriarchy. It provides us with an alternate way of envisioning the Divine and our relationship with Her. It provides brave spaces[13] in which we are encouraged to name our wounds and to claim our power. And it provides us with sacred technologies we can use to heal our hurt places as well as to help others heal theirs.

Why Do We Need to Heal from Patriarchy?

Let's get one thing very clear: No one thrives in a patriarchy. There are people who are more harmed by it – women, other non-men, queer folks, poor folks, people of color, and people living at the intersections of those identities, for a start. But the values that patriarchy upholds – violence, individualism, competition, power-over, just to name a few – take their toll on everyone in the society. Many of us start to do the work of patriarchy ourselves, even if we occupy the most marginalized places in our society.

The wounds of patriarchy for women and other non-men run deep. We are encouraged to make ourselves small, to people please, and to accommodate others at the expense of ourselves. Our intuition and deeper knowings are dismissed as products of mere emotion or fantasy. Our bodies are often not even truly our own, and many of us bear the damage of abuse and violence. All this can leave us feeling very cut off from our power, from ourselves, from our dignity. We become objects rather than agents in our lives. This is a recipe for a host of miseries, large and small, and in our worst moments we reproduce the violence of patriarchy on ourselves and others including our partners, our friends, our children, and pretty much anyone else we come in contact with. Learning to undo the conditioning of patriarchy is a lifelong journey, as is the case with undoing and unlearning any other harmful social conditioning we undergo.

Remember when I said that one of my first mentors in Feminist Witchcraft told me that my first year in the Craft would be all about facing my shit? This is what I am talking about. Fortunately, Feminist Witchcraft provides us with a robust set of tools and frameworks for doing just this.

Witchcraft as a Tool for Reconnection with the Body

One of the greatest wounds inflicted by patriarchy is the severing of the mind from the body. Patriarchal worldviews privilege the mind, along with reason and logic, over the body, intuition, and emotion. It is no accident that mind/reason/logic is associated in much of Western discourse with men and masculinity, and body/intuition/emotion is associated with women and femininity. (And also no accident that these things are set up as yet another binary, with no room for people of a gender outside that binary.) Women and other non-men growing up under patriarchy are systematically taught to devalue and be skeptical of our emotions, of information and wisdom that comes through our bodies, and our emotions. We learn to disregard what our body tells us, and even to seek out embodied experiences at all. When we do seek out embodied experiences, we are encouraged to be objects rather than agents in those activities – performing for the benefit of others, rather than experiencing life for the sake of it. Our bodies are also highly policed under patriarchy – they must be neither too fat or too thin, too broad or too narrow, too sexual or too sexually restrained. We are presented with unattainable standards of physical beauty and then shamed for failing to achieve them. For those who are not cisgender women, the very right of their bodies to exist is questioned. And that's before any religious messages about the sinfulness of the flesh get ahold of us. It is no wonder that we grow up with fraught, sometimes violent, relationships with our bodies.

Feminist Witchcraft offers us an opportunity and a set of tools to use in healing from the body-hate imposed on us by patriarchy. It offers us a chance to reconnect with the body because Witchcraft itself is an *embodied practice* – we experience so much of the Craft via our bodies in ritual, in being in Nature, in being with each other, and in being fully in our bodies. Rather than *believing* in the Goddess, we *experience* Her. Even more importantly, we begin to see Her in ourselves as we allow ourselves to experience our bodies, perhaps for the first time. This can be especially powerful for women and people who are assumed to be women, who have been told that our bodies do not reflect the Divine Order, and are in fact polluted, sinful, or (at best) imperfect copies of a male/masculine God. In contrast, Feminist Witchcraft encourages us to see our bodies as whole, sacred, and worthy just as they are. For some practitioners this can literally mean reframing their relationships to maligned processes such as menstruation, childbirth, and menopause. (In fact, rituals for celebrating these biological and cultural events are a key part of many early texts on Feminist Witchcraft, though focusing solely on such bodily processes can rightfully be critiqued as excluding those who do not experience them.) For other practitioners, making peace with our bodies in terms of their size, our level of ability and disability, eschewing Western beauty standards which cannot be reasonably achieved, or otherwise honoring the body rather than fighting against it are profoundly magickal and healing parts of our journey.

The embodied nature of Feminist Witchcraft reconnects us not just to our physical bodies but to our inherent sacredness and to the wisdom that comes to us through the body. When we learn (or re-learn) body trust, we are able to better trust the myriad ways in which the body is a vehicle for knowledge. This can be learning to trust our intuition – literally, our gut feelings – after a lifetime of being told that we can only have trust in what we know through our rational minds. Fully occupying our body encourages us to connect with our senses, including any "sixth" senses or intuitive/psychic senses we may possess. As we learn to embody our sacredness within our own physical bodies, those bodies become less prisons to escape and more vehicles for fully experiencing the world and connecting to Spirit. Through practices such as dance, bodywork, self-massage, ritual bathing, and drumming – among others – Feminist Witchcraft encourages us to inhabit our bodies and open them as conduits to Divinity and to knowledge and wisdom.

Witchcraft as a Tool for Reconnecting with the Earth

Feminist Witchcraft also provides us with tools for reconnecting with the Earth. Our largely urban, industrialized world, particularly in the West, promotes drastic disconnection from the Earth and the natural world. In many places, especially the US, there are few to no available green spaces for urban dwellers to spend time in nature, and these often are or are perceived to be unsafe spaces. Western culture has also largely promoted the idea that nature is something to be conquered, feared, or extracted from. As a result, many of us spend almost no time in nature, even in heavily managed nature such as parks. Our industrialized food system means that very few of us outside of agricultural areas have a hand in how our food is grown or processed. As a species, we are suffering from nature deficit, and the impacts are real on our physical and mental health.

Although various back-to-nature and environmental movements have questioned it, the dominant worldview of Nature in the West is of an untamed, dangerous, uncivilized vastness to be tamed, feared, and exploited. It is seen as the creation of the Divine, but not sacred within itself. Early writers in the Feminist Spirituality movement noted that Nature is most often coded as feminine and envisioned as a woman in this worldview, and the exploitation of women and the exploitation of Nature mirror one another. Both are wild beings to be tamed by men. Certainly we can and should now expand this discourse to include nor just cisgender women, but all women and other non-men, as well as to recognize the ways in which Black, Brown, and Indigenous people have been exploited along with the Earth itself. (In many cases, this has been done in part by feminizing these groups.) However we might want to parse the gendered nature of the exploitation of the Earth, however, Feminist Witchcraft can offer us a way to reconnect with Nature and our own inherent wildness and sacredness. Many practitioners of Feminist Witchcraft and other Contemporary Pagan movements are deeply concerned with issues of environmental justice as well as gender, racial, and queer justice, and see them (rightfully so) as intertwined. A spirituality that puts the Earth at the center and sees all living beings as extensions of that sacredness allows us to alchemize our environmental consciousness with our own healing, and provides us with a toolkit for both reconnecting with Nature and ourselves.

The lunar cycle, which we'll discuss, provides us with a model for viewing the Earth's cycles reflected in our own lives. As the moon waxes to fullness and then wanes to darkness, so our lives ebb and flow. As mentioned above, many founding Feminist Witches have seen the menstrual cycle and the lunar cycle as reflections of one another, and have created rituals and practices around celebrating menarche, menstruation, and menopause. For those who experience menstruation and have also experienced the social stigmas that come with it, placing these experiences in a sacred context creates a space for reclamation and healing. It is important to remember, however, that not everyone experiences these bodily processes, and not everyone who experiences them sees them as a site for healing and reclamation. It is up to you whether you incorporate your menstrual cycle, or any bodily cycle, into your practice. Even if you choose to simply celebrate the lunar cycle as the cosmic marvel that it is, there is power in reconnecting with this aspect of nature. We are largely an indoor species in modern times, especially at night. Time can go by and become a blur – how many times have you had to ask someone else what day it is? Keeping track of the moon's phases and marking them, however simply, reconnects us to the moon and to the night.

The cycle of Equinoxes, Solstices, and cross-quarter days, which in Contemporary Pagan contexts is typically called the Wheel of the Year, offers us another way to reconnect with Nature by marking it with ritual. The cycles of the Earth mirror the cycles of human life, though it may be hard to find that mirror image in our modern, industrial lifestyles. However, marking the seasonal changes and taking time out to think about the ways our own lives move cyclically can help us feel more a part of the natural order, to feel more grounded, and to feel a greater sense of purpose. Whether you choose to mark these seasonal holidays with elaborate rituals or with something as simple as a walk outside, a moment to take a breath, or a meal of seasonal food, plugging back into Nature and the world around us can be profoundly healing and empowering.

Witchcraft as a Tool for Reconnecting to the Sacred

One of the core wounds that women and other non-men experience at the hands of the patriarchy is disconnection from the Sacred, and by extension from our own sacredness. Being told that we are not created in God's image, and that this justifies the violence and inequality we experience, is a trauma, though many of us only realize this later or never realize it at all. Feminist Witchcraft provides us with alternate visions of what the Sacred, the Divine, God, or whatever your preferred language is for what a good friend of mine calls The Great Cosmic Wow. These alternative visions provide us with ways to see ourselves and people like us reflected in the Divine image, and offer us stories beyond the patriarchal stories of punishment and wrath that so many of us are exposed to starting in childhood.

Religious trauma – what some refer to as "church hurt" – may drive us to avoid engaging in spirituality or with the Sacred at all. While I strongly believe that not everyone needs a spiritual or religious practice to be happy and whole, many of us strongly desire a connection with the Divine but don't know how to find that outside of the patriarchal, monotheistic traditions in which we were raised. Feminist Witchcraft in particular presents us with ways to re-envision the Divine and reconnect with the Sacred through that new vision. While I do not believe, and evidence does not support, that simply having a Goddess makes a religion feminist or liberatory for women, I do believe that being presented with a Divine that looks like us can be. For this to be true, however, we can't just replace the patriarchal God with a Goddess who exhibits similar revenge-based, shame-based, and repressive behaviors. We instead need to be able to envision a drastically different form of Divinity, and part of that drastic difference comes from divorcing the idea of God/Divine/Sacred and exclusive masculinity.

There is no one way to relate to the Goddess within Feminist Witchcraft. Some practitioners relate to Her as a kind of mother figure who is quite directly involved in human affairs. Others might choose particular Goddesses from world mythology that they find interesting, empowering, or compelling. Some may even choose to engage with a male or masculine God alongside the Goddess. Some, like myself, find Goddess imagery useful and healing but don't necessarily think of the Goddess as a distinct being, but instead as more of a universal principle. And some practitioners might choose to find other types of gendered expressions of the Divine that reflect their own life experiences. (One trans friend of mine is a devotee of Aphrodite Urania, the bearded Goddess, for exactly this reason.) The specifics of your relationship with Goddess are personal. What I think is important, and liberatory, about Feminist Witchcraft is that it gives us a *choice* to seek out images and stories of the Sacred that can take us beyond the narrow confines so many of us, especially those raised in the West, have been subject to.

Why do I think this is important? Because finding ways to envision a Divine who looks like us helps us reconnect to our own sacredness. It reminds me that we are all, to borrow a phrase, made in the Divine image. That we are not cut off from the source of life, from the numinous and transcendent. That we are, in fact, the very embodiments of those things. I know that for me, seeing images of Neolithic Goddesses like the Venus of Willendorf, whose soft belly and breasts and rolling curves resembled my own, was the first step in healing the damage that patriarchy and the fatphobia that goes with it had done to me. Seeing myself reflected in the Goddess, and the Goddess reflected in me, *fundamentally changed the way I viewed myself, and the way I treated myself as a result*. While it wasn't as if all the trauma patriarchy had caused me was gone with the snap of a finger (or the wave of a magick wand, if you prefer that image), learning to see myself as an embodiment of the Divine set me on a path to heal that trauma. It's an ongoing journey, even three decades later, but I can trace the beginning to the moment I saw the Venus of Willendorf and the Venus of Laussel in my art history class. It was the first time in my life where I had ever seen my body represented in a way that invited anything but judgement and disgust, and it changed me forever.

When we can reconnect to our own sacredness, we begin to connect to our own power. When we connect to our power, we can learn to stand in that power. And when we can stand in our power, we can transform ourselves and our world. And *that's Witchcraft*.

Chapter 5
Building a Practice

As a *Craft,* Feminist Witchcraft is not just something we believe, but something we *do*. And that practice is intensely personal – while there are some common tools that one finds across Contemporary Witchcraft traditions, in the end each Witch must shape their own practice if it is to be meaningful and sustainable. This chapter provides a framework for building your Feminist Witchcraft practice and offers up some suggestions of tools and techniques you may wish to use as you create a practice that works for you. It is in no way meant to be prescriptive or to put forth the only way to practice Feminist Craft; please take what resonates and leave what doesn't. I do encourage you to experiment with different things as you build your practice. If there are things that you love from other spiritual traditions you've been part of or spiritual practices you have found meaningful, I encourage you to bring those forward into your Craft.

Your Sacred Space

A helpful first step in creating your personal Feminist Witchcraft practice is to set up a designated sacred space for yourself. While Witches tend to believe that all spaces are inherently sacred, creating a dedicated spot in your home is useful as you begin building your practice. A dedicated sacred space can serve as a repository for your spiritual tools (more on those below), a peaceful spot in which to meditate or pray, and a working surface for spellwork and rituals.

The type of sacred space you build is up to you. The size and layout of your living space, the number and ages of the people you live with, whether you have pets, and your personal preferences. It is more important to create a sacred space that works for you than to create one that conforms to some ideal you find in a book, on Instagram or Pinterest, or in another Witch's home. The best sacred space is the one you will use and enjoy on your journey.

Altars

An altar, simply put, is any surface or dedicated area that holds objects that are sacred to you. Altars can be very ornate or quite minimalist, and there is no right or wrong way to construct one. You may choose to create an altar that is up all the time, or you could choose to create a simple altar each time you practice.

An altar can be as simple as a special candle that you choose to light during your practice time, set on a stable surface. Any type of candle will do, though for fire safety, jar candles tend to be my preferred style. If you want to go a little more complicated, placing crystals and stones, images of Goddesses, and other items that are meaningful to you around your central candle are all options. You can choose to leave this altar up at all times – I have a similar set up on my nightstand – or gather the objects from their places in your home each time you want to practice. If leaving your altar up all the time is not an option for you, you might find a pretty basket or other container to keep your items together. One of my favorite traveling altars, for example, is housed in a wooden wine crate. Another, which I take on the go, has small items that travel in a repurposed Altoids tin.

There are no rules about what you should keep on your altar. If you are coming from a tradition such as Wicca, where specific tools such as an athame (ritual knife) or chalice are typically placed on the altar, you can feel free to continue to use that set up. I personally do not keep my working tools on my altar all the time – I find it makes the space cluttered – but other Witches like to have everything close at hand. Some things you might wish to have on your altar include:

- Representations of the five Elements – Earth, Air, Fire, Water, and Spirit. You might use a candle for each Element, placed in its cardinal direction. (The most typical alignment is Earth/North, Air/East, Fire/South, Water/West, and Spirit/Center). Alternatively, you can choose other items that represent the Elements to you. For instance, crystals and stones for Earth; feathers or incense for Air; candles for Fire; a dish of water or seashells for Water; crystals or a bell for Spirit. Feel free to get creative! If you come from a cultural tradition that aligns the Elements differently than I have described above, please feel free to substitute!
- A central candle. This can be the candle that you light during your spiritual practice. I recommend a jar candle of some kind for fire safety purposes. A simple white jar candle that you can find in many supermarkets works great, but a pretty scented jar candle from your favorite home store is also a solid choice. Never leave a burning candle unattended! (Having matches or a lighter and a candle snuffer handy is also a good idea.)
- Representations of Goddess. While there is a great deal of beautiful Goddess statuary on the market, don't feel you need to rush out and purchase any before you build your altar. Choose items that represent Goddess as you know Her. I collect Paleolithic and Neolithic inspired Goddess figures such as replicas of the Venus of Willendorf. But I also have a vinyl figurine of the comic book character Red Sonja on my altar, because she evokes Goddess's warrior face to me. A friend of mine has a figure of Wonder Woman on her altar, to remind herself of her own power. Another friend doesn't use human-looking figures at all, but represents Goddess on their altar with a large cowrie shell.

- Elements from Nature. Stones, crystals, shells, and feathers are common items found on altars, but anything that connects you to the Earth and is meaningful to you can go on your altar. A dear friend of mine keeps both a shed snakeskin and a spent wasp nest on their altar, as these were found on nature walks and felt like gifts. Fresh or dried flowers, a potted plant, a dish of soil from a place special to you, or water from a body of water that feels sacred to you might also find places on your altar.

As always, these are only suggestions. Trust your intuition. Know that an altar is a living thing and will change over time. In the nearly three decades of my own practice (as of this writing), I have had everything from a single candle and a couple of crystals to a full blown working Wiccan altar with a complete set of tools, and now I'm working with a very simple altar of Goddess figures and crystals.

Finally, remember that even though altars and spiritual tools are wonderful, they are not necessary for you to commune with Goddess or to create powerful Witchcraft. The only altar you ever truly need is yourself, and you hold the sacred within you. Your heart, mind, and intention are more powerful than any item you can purchase.

Building a Practice

Your sacred space can serve as a focus spot as you build your practice. It is not necessary to spend hours each day meditating in front of your altar or lighting candles. I do think it's worth your time to regularly take a moment to stand before your altar or handle your sacred objects, using this time as an opportunity to connect to yourself and to the Divine. Your life will determine what "regularly" means. For some people this might be every day. But it's also fine if you find that your life only allows you to spend focused time at your altar on the Full or New Moons (more about those in a later chapter), or if the only time you have to yourself is on Tuesdays for 30 minutes. The section that follows contains some suggested techniques that you can experiment with as you build your own Feminist Witchcraft practice. This list is by no means exhaustive, and you do not have to incorporate all of these techniques into your practice.

Meditation

Cultivating a meditation habit can serve as a cornerstone of your practice. The word *meditation* can be intimidating to those who've never done it, as it can conjure up images of monks sitting in silence for hours or twisting one's self into a lotus pose. But meditation can be very simple, as simple as paying attention to your breathing for a few minutes. A full course in meditation is far beyond the scope of this book, but I encourage you to experiment with meditation and mindfulness techniques as you build your Feminist Witchcraft practice. Spending just a few minutes in meditation a day, or at least with some regularity, provides an opportunity to slow down and connect. My favorite simple meditation is simply to light a candle and sit down in front of my altar and *just breathe* for five minutes. My mind doesn't magickly become quiet, but I remind myself to let the thoughts flow. I set a timer on my phone and when the chime goes off, more often than not I feel more connected and centered.

Prayer

Prayer is another term that many Witches and Contemporary Pagans might approach with skepticism. It can remind us of the spiritual traditions we were brought up with, which does not always call up happy memories. However, prayer in one form or another can be an excellent way to connect with the Divine or to simply slow down and pay attention. Prayer does not have to involve supplication or debasing oneself before Deity. I tend to approach prayer as a kind of conversation with Goddess – it's my chance to speak with the sacred as I know it, and to listen for answers. Even a simple prayer of gratitude can change the energy of your day. You can also incorporate affirmations into your prayer practice if you like.

Divination

Divination is a common practice among many Witches, and can take many forms: Tarot card, oracle cards, pendulums, Lenormand cards, runes, and a seemingly endless list of other tools and techniques. A brief daily (or otherwise regular) divination practice can serve as a wonderful tool for connection and spiritual growth. A simple practice I have employed for years is pulling a single oracle or Tarot card at the start of the day to get a sense of what the day might bring. Another way to incorporate divination into your everyday practice is to choose a Goddess-themed oracle deck and draw a different card each day, as a way to learn about various Goddesses. If you prefer to work with other divination tools such a pendulum or runes, taking the time to do a brief reading on a regular basis can be a simple yet grounding exercise. I sometimes struggle with my freeform divination practice, and have found a little structure can help me get back on track. You can find daily Tarot or Oracle challenges on Instagram and other social media that offer prompts for each day. Even if you don't choose to post your daily divination to social media, these can be helpful and fun.

Journaling

The idea of keeping a journal can be daunting if you've never done it, as we often associate the idea of journaling with the belief we have to keep a detailed daily record of our lives. But journaling can be a great way to connect with yourself, ground, and otherwise explore your feelings and your spiritual practice. There is no right or wrong way to keep a journal, however. Taking the time to write just a few sentences to start or close out your day can be a powerful ritual. I have a small journal that prompts me to write down one to three sentences per day, and I am amazed at how centering this is. If the idea of free form journaling is intimidating to you, I recommend using journal prompts. You can find these on social media and Goddess-centered blogs, and there are also a number of journals that contain prompts as well. You could also choose to blog or use social media as a journal, or just type in a simple Word document. And you don't have to limit yourself to writing – drawing, collaging, and other forms of art journaling "count" too. A friend of mine uses voice memos in her phone for reflections on her daily divination practice rather than committing them to paper or hard drive.

Intentional Movement

One of the things I love most about Feminist Witchcraft and Goddess Spirituality broadly is how embodied it is. Incorporating intentional movement into your practice can help foster healthy connection with your body and your own inner Divinity. Finding an intentional movement practice that feels good and that honors your body is a powerful way to honor Goddess and to honor your own sacredness.

When exploring intentional movement, first and foremost respect your body – you do not need to do anything rigorous or that goes beyond what your body can do at a given moment. I incorporate a lot of dance and meditative movement in my own practice; a dear circle sister of mine who uses a wheelchair sometimes practices with me by moving her arms and hands in beautiful patterns while I twirl around the room. She has found a way to incorporate movement and connection with me in a way that also honors her own body. Some forms of intentional movement you might want to explore include, but are not limited to the following.

- *Dance*. I love to dance, and dancing in ritual circles and at festivals has been a huge source of healing for me. Though I have some training as a modern dancer, the dance I use in my spiritual practice is much more free form, letting my body move in ways that feel good and that connect to the music or drumming I'm listening to. Allowing your body to move or sway along with music can be a gentle way to introduce dance into your practice, especially if you are at all self-conscious about dancing. You might also explore belly dance (being mindful of issues of cultural appropriation), trance and ecstatic dance such as Gabrielle Roth's Five Rhythms, or a dance form that is grounded in your own culture. Don't limit yourself. You're just as likely to find me dancing to heavy metal as to drums or Goddess chants!
- *Yoga*. Another way I like to start my day is by doing a short series of yoga poses to wake up my body and to center my spirit. I've been practicing yoga much of my adult life, but I return to very simple poses when I start my day. You do not need to be super flexible or have a certain body shape to do yoga – every body is a yoga body! Learning a few gentle poses via a class, a YouTube video, or a yoga app is a great way to start. There are many different styles of yoga and all poses can be modified to work with your body and range of motion.
- *Walking Meditations*. If you have difficulty sitting still to meditate, a walking meditation can be a great way to incorporate both meditation and intentional movement into your life. My favorite type of walking meditation is walking a labyrinth, but that's not always possible with a busy schedule. A short walk around your block or through a local park can be a sacred experience if you allow yourself to focus on the natural world around you. In the heat of a Texas summer, when it was too hot to

go out, I've even used my treadmill time as a walking meditation!

You should also feel free to experiment with other types of intentional movement, including tai chi or other martial arts, stretching, forms of exercise that you enjoy – I've definitely used my time in the gym or the pool as a time to work on the health of my spirit as well as my body – or anything else that feels right to you. Maybe your moving meditation is to spend some time on your kids' swingset in the backyard, to wash your dishes, or to dig in your flower beds. Any movement done with awareness and intention can be a part of your practice.

Build a Practice That's Yours

The forms your regular practice takes aren't nearly as important as building a practice that feels right to you. While I have given you some suggestions in the preceding pages, you will ultimately be the one to decide what works best for you and feels authentic. As you read further into Feminist Witchcraft and explore the writings of other practitioners, and as you meet others and enter community (if you so choose), you'll encounter all sorts of ideas about what regular practice can look like. I encourage you to experiment and try things out. I also encourage you to think about the things that are important to you in your life, and to consider treating them as sacred too. For instance, as I am typing this chapter, I am thinking of my fingers flying over the keyboard as sacred movement, and of the finished product as a gift to community and to Goddess. If you are a cook or a baker, perhaps your time in the kitchen becomes infused with sacredness and intention.

Also know that your practice will change over time. When we first begin, we are typically full of enthusiasm and want to try *all the things*. But life can also get in the way – modern life keeps us so occupied and distracted – and you might realize that a detailed morning practice that worked for you at one point is now incompatible with your life, or with the season of your life. For those of us raised in the religious traditions dominant in the West, this can bring with it a sense of shame or of being a "bad" practitioner. Be gentle with yourself if your practice slips or changes over time, or if you need to take a break to attend to life's matters – remember that it's all sacred! You may also find over time that different practices take on meaning for you, or that you outgrow some practices that were once important to you. This is also OK. We are meant to grow and to change, and our practice will grow and change along with it.

Chapter 6
Ritual

The word *ritual* gets a bad rap in much of Western culture, as it tends to call up images of either distant and exotic people doing distant and exotic things or, worse, images drawn from horror movies of people engaged in unspeakable behavior in honor of some dark being. While, yes, technically those are both examples of ritual, there's much more to ritual than either of these sets of images portrays.

Anthropologically speaking (I did warn you I'm an anthropologist, right?), ritual is simply a set of repetitive behaviors that are different from the behaviors of everyday life. By this definition, the simple practices we talked about in Chapter 5 are their own forms of ritual. Ritual at its most basic is time we set aside to simply be and do something different from what we do the rest of the time, to be present in the moment.

Feminist Witchcraft and Ritual

Feminist Witches use ritual for a variety of reasons: to celebrate the passage of the Earth's seasons, to honor the cycles of the Moon, to mark significant life events and transitions, and to build sacred community – just to name a few. Those of us who grew up within mainstream Western culture have lived lives largely devoid of community ritual, and as such we often find we have a hunger to create sacred space and time, to mark life stages, to collectively celebrate and mourn and speak our truth. Feminist Witchcraft ritual was designed with this deep cultural need in mind, and offers us an avenue to get that need met. Ritual also meets our need to take time out, to take a breath, and to spend time in the presence of the Sacred – all of which help us to be healthier, happier, and more balanced.

As with the process of building your daily or regular practice, your relationship with ritual will be personal and can be developed in a way that makes sense for you and your life. Some Witches like full-blown ceremonies with lots of candles and incense smoke, flowing robes, and everything you might picture when you hear the word *ritual*. Others prefer something simpler and more low-key, such as setting aside time each Full Moon to sit outside and meditate. And most Witches I've known, myself included, tend towards something in the middle of these two poles. There is no right or wrong way to do ritual or to build a ritual practice. There are some common elements and ritual cycles that you are likely to encounter within the Witchcraft community at large and within Feminist Witchcraft communities and gatherings specifically, however. You can adopt some, all, or none of these into your own practice. I'll share a bit of what has worked for me and that I've found meaningful, as well as some practices and ideas about ritual that I've encountered that, while I haven't adopted them myself, have proven meaningful for other Witches. Consider this something of a smorgasbord, rather than something set down in stone.

Elements of Feminist Witchcraft Ritual

Feminist Witchcraft ritual is an immensely flexible thing, but there are some common elements you are likely to encounter especially if you attend gatherings, open rituals, or Feminist Witchcraft festivals. You will see some overlap with the ideas presented in the previous chapter, and those of you familiar with Wicca and other forms of Contemporary Paganism may also see many commonalities in what follows. As always, incorporate what works for you into your practice, and feel no pressure to adopt what doesn't. The basic format I use for my rituals is below – I invite you to use all or parts of it!

Basic Ritual Format

Create sacred space

Call the circle

State the purpose of the ritual

Raise energy

Works of magick or spellwork

Grounding activity

Opening the circle

Creating Sacred Space

Generally speaking, Feminist Witches do not have churches, temples, or other designated places where we go to practice; rather, we practice in our homes, out in nature, or in locations that serve multiple functions. While to a Goddess- and Earth-centered person everyplace is inherently sacred, it helps our brains and bodies slip into a ritual mindset when we take time to demarcate a sacred space before we begin. In Feminist Witchcraft, this is most often done through a practice called *casting a circle*.

Why a circle? Circles (along with other techniques for creating sacred space) create what anthropologist Arnold Van Gennep called "liminal space" – spaces that are between worlds or states of being. Circles are non-hierarchical – everyone in the circle is on equal footing. Circles also provide for interconnection. Everyone in the circle is connected and plays a part in facilitating that connection. If you are engaging in magick or spellwork (more on that in the next chapter), the circle also serves as an energetic container for that work. And even if you are alone within your circle, it provides a space where you are connected to the Goddess.

Before you cast a circle, it's a good idea to do some sort of energetic cleansing of the space – as well as a quick physical cleanse with a broom or vacuum if needed. Burning incense or cleansing herbs and wafting the smoke through the space is a common practice for cleansing space. While herbs such as white sage and palo santo are popular in many Witchcraft communities for cleansing, I avoid them in my own practice due to issues of sustainability and cultural appropriation. Each Witch has to make their own decision about this, and for me it has made sense to explore other herbs with which I have a geographical or historical connection, such as garden sages, wild mugwort, juniper, and rosemary. Salt water is also a common cleansing agent for creating sacred space. Sweeping the area with a broom that is used only for ritual purposes can feel delightfully witchy as well.

Casting a circle can be an ornate process or a simple one, depending on your personality and the occasion for which you are creating sacred space. Some people like to outline the circle with chalk or rope in order to create a physical demarcation. Others – including me – prefer to simply walk in a circle in the chosen area and imagine the circle being created with each step. If you are doing ritual alone, you can even silently visualize the circle surrounding you.

Honoring the Directions/Elements

As we saw in the previous chapter, a recognition of the cardinal directions – North, South, East, and West – and their associated Elements is a common feature of Feminist Witchcraft practice. The most common alignment of the directions and the elements draws from the Western occult tradition, which has heavily influenced contemporary Witchcraft of all kinds. The alignment I use in my own practice is:

- North/Earth
- East/Air
- South/Fire
- West/Water
- Center/Spirit

Some Witches build a special altar at each of the directions, while others simply include representations on the central altar. I tend to decide which way to go based on what the ritual is for, if there is a group circling with me, where I am conducting ritual, and my intuition at the time.

The Altar

An altar in the center of the circle, or in one of the cardinal directions, is customary for Feminist Witchcraft ritual. As with the altar you create for your daily or regular practice, this can be as simple or as ornate as you wish. If you are creating an altar for one of the seasonal celebrations, you might add fruits or flowers of the season. An altar for a specific Goddess could include images of Her or traditional or intuited offerings to Her. A ritual to honor a loved one who has passed away could feature pictures and mementos. One of my favorite experiences in my Feminist Witchcraft journey has always been watching the way that people spontaneously build communal altars when we get together; this communal altar building can be a powerful part of group ritual as well.

A simple altar might feature a stone (for Earth), a feather (for Air), a candle (for Fire), a cup or bowl of water (for Water), a crystal (for Spirit), and a representation of the Goddess. That might mean an actual statue or image, a candle, a flower, or anything else that you feel represents the Goddess as you know Her. On a practical note, if you plan to light candles or incense, having matches or a lighter, along with a way to quickly extinguish flames, is a good idea.

Calling the Circle

Once you have your space and your altar set up, the ritual begins with what I and many other Feminist Witches call *calling the circle*. This is the time when you welcome the Elements and the Goddess, state any intentions you might have for the ritual, and otherwise complete the creation of your sacred space. Once you have called the circle (sometimes also known as *closing the circle*), the heart of the ritual can begin.

You will find many different circle calls in books and online, and of course, you may write your own. It is sometimes useful to read and try what others have written as inspiration for your own. You can also welcome the Elements and the Goddess silently in your heart – which is what I often do when doing ritual by myself. When I am doing ritual with a group, my standard circle call looks something like this (though I also improvise a LOT depending on my mood and the occasion).

Circle Call

Welcome to the Spirits of the North, Element of Earth
Abundance, healing, the Earth beneath our feet
The strength of our bones
Welcome

Welcome to the Spirits of the East, Element of Air
Communication, inspiration, intellectual knowledge
The breath in our lungs
Welcome

Welcome to the Spirits of the South, Element of Fire
Creativity, passion, catalyst for change
The fire in our bellies
Welcome

Welcome to the Spirits of the West, Element of Water
Healing, spirituality, emotion
The ocean upon which we enter the world
Welcome

Welcome the Spirits of the Center, Element of Spirit
Animating spark, life force, unifying energy
That which brings together everything
Welcome

We welcome the Goddess
In the forms in which we know Her
She of 1000 faces and 1000 names
Welcome

[ring bell three times]

By the Earth that is our bodies,
By the Air that is our breath,
By the Fire of our bright spirits,
And by the Water of our blood, sweat, and tears,
The circle is cast
We stand in a place between the worlds
What is between the worlds can change the worlds
And what can change the worlds is us[14]

The Body of the Ritual

Once you have called the circle, you have entered the body of the ritual. There is really no set format for the body of a ritual in Feminist Witchcraft – because ritual is immensely flexible, and because Feminist Witchcraft encourages practitioners to create rituals that meet their individual and group needs, every ritual will look different. There are many anthologies of rituals out there to provide you with inspiration, and I encourage you to explore them.

The body of ritual is where you will be doing the "work" the ritual is designed for – celebrating a sacred day, raising healing energy for someone, honoring the Moon, dedicating yourself to a particular Goddess, you name it. Because creating ritual is work, I encourage you to always have a purpose for doing so, even if that purpose is as simple as providing a sacred container for storytelling, community building, or celebration. If you are crafting a ritual that will include spellwork, which we will discuss in the next chapter, then it is even more important that you have a sense of purpose before you begin.

I like to state my purpose clearly when I start ritual. That might be "We are gathered here to celebrate the Full Moon" or "I am here to do a healing spell for my friend who has asked for support during her illness" or even "We come together tonight to share our stories and work for an end to gender based violence." Stating your purpose helps your brain – and the minds of anyone else in the ritual circle with you – to focus clearly on the intent of the ritual.

After stating the purpose of your ritual, the actual format can vary a great deal. Generally speaking, I refer to this as the "energy raising" stage, as we are working to direct our energy toward the intent or goal of the ritual. Oftentimes this includes reading or reciting of poems or stories, sharing information about the holiday being celebrated or the cause being advocated for, the retelling of myths and sacred stories. For instance, each one of my public Full Moon rituals includes a brief discussion of the theme of the moon and the astrological forces at work. A healing ritual for a friend might include sharing stories about them. You get the idea.

Raising energy within ritual can take a variety of forms. The goal is to focus on the intent or goal of the ritual, raise energy, and direct that energy towards that goal or intent. Some of the ways that I have raised energy in ritual include:

- Chanting or singing
- Dancing
- Meditating, guided or freeform

- Tying knots (especially useful for rituals around binding or creating)
- Drumming
- Harmonized breathing
- Meditating
- Working on a collective artwork

As you build your practice, you are likely to learn which types of energy raising you enjoy and which work for your body. Bring these into your rituals. A good friend of mine finds knitting meditative and thus uses it as part of her energy raising in ritual. Another is a belly dancer, and uses simple dance moves and beats when she creates ritual. A former coven sister of mine who lived with chronic pain often used music and swaying hand and upper body movements in lieu of dancing. Experiment!

What do you do with all that energy once it's raised? You direct it towards the intention of the ritual. This might involve holding (and passing around) a candle that's being charged for a loved one's healing, or visualizing a cause or issue and then visualizing the energy raised going toward resolving that issue or supporting those working for the cause. For instance, as part of a ritual I took part in in support of the Black Lives Matter movement in the United States, we raised energy by reading the names of those who had been killed by law enforcement and repeating them, and with the energy raised by our voices directed them to the protestors in our city who were working for justice. (We also donated to the cause and worked as community educators.)

Grounding

After you've sent that energy on its way, you will need to come down a bit. In Witchcraft, we call this *grounding* and, as the name implies, it's meant to bring you back down to Earth. Traditionally, Witches ground with food and drink – something called *cakes and ale* or *the simple feast* in more Wicca-oriented groups. This is a simple meal (more like a snack) of bread and a beverage – wine and mead are common, with apple juice or grape juice being frequent nonalcoholic alternatives. In my rituals, we eat chocolate to bring us back into our bodies. The foods you choose for grounding can be based on the season or the ritual's intent. One of my favorite takes on the simple feast was in a ritual designed to heal the inner child, and the priestess in charge offered us cookies and milk – with soy milk and vegan cookies available for those who needed that.

You may also choose to ground without food and drink. This is especially if you are doing ritual with a large group of people whose dietary needs you are not certain of, such as leading a ritual at a festival or gathering. In this case, asking people to *ground the energy* by touching the floor or Earth is a good alternative. You can use this practice in your smaller or solo rituals as well.

Opening the Circle

The final step in a Feminist Witchcraft ritual is *opening the circle* – essentially doing what you did to call the circle in reverse. This helps to transform the sacred space back to mundane space, to mark the end of the active part of the ritual, and to signal to our brains that it's time to come out from between the worlds.

The first step is to thank the Goddess in the forms you welcomed Her or in which She showed up in the ritual. Then it is customary to bid farewell to the Elements. Many Witches I know open their circle by using the same language they used to welcome the Elements, substituting farewell language for welcome language. You can do this counterclockwise (West-South-East-North) if you wish, or in the same order you welcomed the Elements. The Element of Spirit is usually dismissed first, right after thanking the Goddess. My favorite way to bid farewell to the Elements and open my circle is below, and is something I learned at a festival many years ago:

Opening the Circle

West, South, East, North
Thanks to those that we've called forth
Water, Fire, Air, Earth
Return you now
To Gaia's girth
The circle is open![15]

Much like building a personal regular practice, building a ritual practice takes time. Unlike Contemporary Pagan traditions, Feminist Witchcraft does not have a set liturgical calendar. There are some Feminist Witches, myself included, that follow a seasonal calendar that resembles the Wiccan calendar and which we'll explore in a later chapter. Others (including me) also honor the Moon phases, which will also explore soon. However, because Feminist Witchcraft is deeply personal and is at the heart about your own healing and growth, you can choose your own structure for how often and why you engage in ritual.

Ritual can be elaborate or it can be simple. What matters is that we make time for it. Why? Because ritual speaks to a different part of our brains that the activities of ordinary life. It creates a time that is set aside for us to be in the presence of the Sacred, however we define that. It allows the part of our brain that wants to engage with symbols and make free associations time to play. Ritual also gives us a way to mark the passage of sacred time, to honor life phases and events, and to build a time for experiencing our emotions into our lives. And it's a crucible for transformation. We're always a little different coming out of a ritual than we were going in, even if the change is subtle. And what's not magickal about that?

And speaking of *magick*...let's turn to the subject of spellwork.

Chapter 7

Magick and Spellcraft

So, big philosophical questions and theological explorations are great, but isn't Witchcraft about actually *doing things*? Absolutely! Witchcraft is a *Craft* – it is something we do; it is an act of creation. While some people may find power in simply venerating Goddess, I would argue that without the practice of ritual and Witchcraft, those folks are not Feminist Witches – they are Goddess Spirituality practitioners, and that's good and valid and beautiful. To be a Witch of any stripe, it is necessary to practice. That practice can look a lot of different ways, but it is above all *active rather than passive.*

Up to this point, we've talked a lot about history, politics, and ritual mechanics. What we haven't talked much about is the thing so many people associate with Witchcraft – magick and spells. This is by design. While the idea of being able to do magick or use spells to influence the world is what attracts many people to Contemporary Witchcraft traditions, I believe that it's important to have a strong foundation in the Craft before you move into this area. Some of the first magick we do in Feminist Witchcraft is the alchemical work of healing ourselves, and until we get comfortable doing that, I don't believe we have any business trying to influence the larger world. I also believe that spells and magick should be our tools of last resort in most cases, as part of reclaiming your power and healing yourself from the wounds of patriarchy is learning how to problem-solve, have faith in your ability to find solutions through channels both mundane and esoteric, and rely on yourself to navigate through life's ups and downs.

But sometimes we need a little extra help, help that can't be found in our everyday world. And that's where magick and spellcraft come in.

What Do We Mean by "Magick"?

Witchcraft involves the practice of magick – let's get that out of the way, for those who were wondering – but magickal practice is not the sum total of what it is to practice Witchcraft, at least not in Feminist Craft as I know and practice it.

Magick, as Starhawk has said, is the act of changing consciousness at will. I add to this that it is the act of changing consciousness at will *in order to effect change in the outer and/or inner world*. While not all people who practice magick consider themselves Witches, and not all magick is Witchcraft, magick is a key element of Feminist Witchcraft. The desire to effect change in the outside world, and within our inner worlds to help us heal from the damage of the patriarchy, underlies much of magickal worked in Feminist Witchcraft spaces.

What do I mean when I call magick a change in consciousness? I mean that magick is a skill that allows us to move easily from a mundane consciousness – the consciousness we use in our everyday lives – to a consciousness that allows us to see the connections between things and thus to impact them. In many ways, I think of this as a liminal consciousness. We are able to impact our inner and even outer reality when we are able to shift consciousness in this way. It may not be as exciting as being able to wiggle your nose or snap your fingers to grant your own wish, but magick of this type is an exercise in power. That's why we wield it carefully.

Spellcraft

While you may sometimes hear the terms *magick* and *spellcraft* used interchangeably, there are subtle and important differences. Magick is the act of changing consciousness. Spellcraft (or simply *spells*) is what you do once you've made that shift in consciousness. To put it simply, all spells are magick, but not all magick is a spell. Spells involve using materials, chosen based on correspondences, in the service of magick. Think of candles, stones, herbs...even eye of newt, though you won't find that in most modern spellbooks.

Although spells tend to involve a lot of *stuff*, it's key to remember that that stuff has no inherent magickal power. While there are items that have been endowed with a lot of power via cultural tradition – think candles, herbs known for specific properties, and salt, to name a few – their power comes from belief. Simply lighting a green candle, for instance, is unlikely to get you a job interview; lighting a green candle, speaking your intention over it, and taking practical action on your job search has a much higher chance of success. Especially here in the 21st century, when Witchcraft is being commoditized like everything else, there are people who will want to sell you special, "enchanted," or "powerful" items on the open marketplace. Know that it is not necessary to purchase special items to engage in effective spellwork – Feminist Witchcraft especially encourages us to use what we have at hand, to think in terms of sustainability, and to reject the excesses of capitalism where and how we can. Go ahead and buy that neat candle for your banishing spell, but know that you don't need it for your magick to work.

Magickal Ethics

With great power, as we know, comes great responsibility. Media portrayals and cautionary tales about Witchcraft would have it that Witches are out there, hexing willy-nilly and using magick to solve all our problems. I am sure there are Witches out there doing just that –I've met them – but as a general rule that's not how Feminist Witches operate. (Remember what I said about spells and magick being a tool of last resort?) As such, it's important to develop a code of ethics around your use of spells and magick.

Here is where many of you are probably expecting me to invoke what Wiccans call The Law of Three – that what we put out to the universe returns to us three times, and thus we should avoid any potentially harmful spellwork. Well, I am not going to do that. You are, of course, welcome to embrace The Law of Three in your practice if you would like, but it's far from compulsory. For as much as I disagree with her about many things, I am more in line with what Z. Budapest has said about magickal ethics – that a Witch who cannot hex, cannot heal. I interpret this to mean that when we learn a particular form of magick, we also learn its shadow side or its reversal, and to tap into our own power, we must be able to wield both. We need to decide in any given moment whether the potential harm or unintended effects of our spellworking are worth the potential gain. When we are clear about our own values and principles – as we will be, if we have been doing the work of healing from patriarchy – we have a solid ethical code that can guide our practice.

I do not use The Law of Three in my own practice because it feels fear-based to me. I always feel as though I'm being threatened with a wrist slap or worse from the Divine if I step out of bounds with my spellwork. Having come from, and having had to do a lot of healing from, a fear-based theology in which I was raised, I don't want to recreate that. I believe that I can trust my own instincts and moral compass to do what's right without threat of karmic or divine retribution.

That said, I use spellwork judiciously, and almost never to solve my own personal problems. I am more likely to draw on my inner power and confidence to navigate life's various currents. Where I do tend to use spellwork is when I am working with a group, most often around social justice issues, and building a spell together is a way for us to align and bring our energy into harmony around the cause we are fighting for.

A Note on Hexing and Baneful Magicks

While I do not subscribe to the Law of Three, I am also not an advocate of using hexes or other baneful magicks to solve problems unless there is no other alternative. Part of learning to know yourself and to know your power is to know how to choose the right tool for the job. Most of the time, there is a way to use spellwork to solve or aid a problem without causing harm to others. But sometimes there's not, and that can be especially true for spells around social justice issues. There are times when the harm committed by the spell will offset the much larger harm at hand. For instance, I had no qualms about engaging in the collective hexing of certain political figures. While the hex could have harmed them, the fact that they were harming so many people themselves evened the balance for me. I don't think we could have blessed those people into behaving better. It was worth at least attempting to ameliorate or limit the harm to bystanders who had done no wrong.

Not every Feminist Witch I knew agreed with me on that, and that's fine with me. It's your mileage on issues such as The Law of Three, hexing or baneful spells, and how to determine what is ethical or not in your own practice. What's important is that you develop your own code of magickal ethics that you can live by. And it's important to communicate those to anyone you might do ritual or spellwork with, so you can be on the same page.

Creating Spells

While there are acres of spellbooks available, I tend to create a spell from scratch when I use one. I might look at books or online for inspiration, but I don't tend to use anyone else's spells verbatim. Instead, I follow a pretty simple formula when creating my own spells:

- Set the intent
- Gather the items
- Charge the items
- Send the energy on its way

This formula has worked well for me whether I'm using candle magick, knot magick, poppet (doll) magick, or any other method. A full discussion of all those types of magick is beyond the scope of this book, so let's walk through a simple candle spell as an example of how my formula works.

Set the Intent

Good Witches know that intent is the strongest magick. Just using your intent directed towards a goal can sometimes bring about results. (Some people refer to this as *manifesting*.) Knowing what you want the outcome of a spell to be is hugely important before you take the time and energy to engage in the actual spellwork.

For example, several of my fellow Feminist Witches and I organized in 2024 around an anti-transgender bill in our state. While our overarching goal for society is to be rid of transphobia and to live in a country where trans folks have equality, that was going to be too big of a lift for a single spell. Instead we focused our intent on *this particular bill not passing through the legislature and being signed by the governor*. It gave us a clear target – we had the bill number and were able to read it online, we knew when it was being debated and voted on, and stopping it would be a victory and a step towards a more trans-affirming state.

Think specific when you set your intent whenever possible. Especially when we are doing spellwork around social justice issues, it can be tempting to go for the big overarching goal. But choosing something discrete helps you narrow your focus.

Gather the Items

I decided that my contribution to our collective work to stop the bill would be a candle spell. I looked in my candle stash (don't judge), and I found a white candle set with carnelian chips that a friend of mine had given me. Carnelian is known as a stone that helps with legal matters. Then I thought about what else would symbolize justice to me. I gathered the Justice cards from three of my Tarot decks. I also added statues of the aspects of The Morrigan, a Goddess I feel connected to and who works against injustice. I added a figure of the Greek Goddess Athena, known for her wise judgement, as well. I also grabbed a box of matches.

Charge the Items

Once I gathered my items, I set up a small altar in my sacred space. I placed the Tarot cards and the Goddess figures in a configuration that was pleasing to me. Then I took the candle in my hands, as it would be the star of the show. I held the candle in my hands for a few moments while breathing deeply. In my mind, I saw the bill failing. I saw the headlines in the next day's newspaper announcing that it would not become law. As I visualized, I imagined those images going into the candle.

When I was ready, I said:

With this candle, I light the Lamp of Justice
May you light the way
May the Trans Erasure Bill fail
May there be legislators of conscience
Who prevent this from becoming law
May this be a step towards a more affirming and equal state
May you light the way

Sending your energy into items such as the candle is known as *charging* and I think of it like powering the items up.

When I felt like the candle was well charged, I lit it.

Send the Energy on Its Way

Once the candle was lit, I placed it on the altar I had built. I let it burn for a few hours while I worked in the same room, and each time I looked at it, I went back to my visualization about the bill failing. I burned the candle for a time each day and repeated the visualization until the day of the vote came. (I never leave burning candles unattended – I feel that it's perfectly sensible to extinguish a candle and relight it later.)

The bill? It failed.

A Final Word on Spellcraft

I know some of my readers will be disappointed I do not include a compendium of spells in this chapter. But I think it's incredibly important to learn to create your own spells. It helps us find the magick in the everyday. For instance, a sister Witch of mine will write the things she is banishing from her life and flush them down the toilet because it symbolizes that she is *sick of that shit* and sending it away from her. When I was first exploring warrior Goddesses, a dear friend gave me a vinyl sculpture of the graphic novel character Red Sonya, complete with chainmail bikini and sword. She sits right next to my more conventional Goddess figures, and she comes out on the altar during any spellwork I do around gender justice. Neither of these things are conventional and probably won't be found in any published spellbooks, but they are tangible forms of magick to us.

I encourage you to play around with the spellcrafting formula I've laid out above and see what you can come up with.

Find your magick. Find your Power. Be the Witch you were born to become.

Chapter 8
Special Days

Throughout this book, I've mentioned that there are two calendars of special days that Feminist Witches may choose to honor. This chapter discusses them in brief. You may choose to honor all, some, or none of these days. You may also wish to celebrate various Goddess feast days, significant days in history, or days of personal significance. If you enter into Feminist Witchcraft or broader Contemporary Pagan community, you are likely to see these days marked with rituals or other formal celebrations, so it's good to have a grasp of the basics.

The Lunar Cycle

The Moon has been associated with the Goddess and with things designated as "feminine" in Western culture for millennia. And the Moon has been associated with Witches for just about as long. Early writers in Feminist Spirituality and Feminist Witchcraft made the connection between the Moon and the cycles of menstruation, and you will find much writing on this topic. I think we can honor the Moon with or without making any correlations with bodily processes. But I do love tapping into the power of the Moon in my practice.

The Moon completes Her cycle approximately every 28–29 days. Each year features 12 Full Moons, with some years featuring a thirteenth or "Blue" Moon. As the Moon works Her way through the lunar cycle, Her energies change along with her visibility. Choosing to coordinate our spiritual and magickal working with the Moon can bring extra power and connection to that work.

Stages of the Lunar Cycle

For our purposes, we will be working with four phases of the lunar cycle. This is a simplified way to look at the cycle, and those who are interested in bringing planetary and astrological influences into their work can look more deeply into the various phases of the Moon between the major ones we'll discuss here. We'll be looking at the New Moon, the Waxing Moon, the Full Moon, and the Waning Moon.

The New Moon marks the beginning of a new lunar cycle. The moon is not visible in the sky at this time. Because it is the beginning of a new cycle for the Moon, this is a great time to put things into motion, to set intentions for the next lunar cycle or around a particular project, to declare a fresh start, and to plant seeds (physical or metaphorical). The New Moon gives us a chance to pause – it is that space between one thing ending and the next thing beginning.

As the New Moon moves through the sky, She grows more visible. This stage is known as the Waxing Moon. Those intentions you set at the New Moon are growing along with the Moon Herself. Use the Waxing Moon when there are things you want to see increase – money magicks, fertility, abundance. The Moon waxes for about two weeks, until She becomes full.

The Full Moon is the midpoint in the lunar cycle. The image of Witches dancing under the Full Moon isn't a cliche for nothing! Full Moons are times of celebration, of community, and for doing ritual and spellwork intended to affect change. Full Moons are also an ideal time for releasing things from your life, as the Moon begins to become less visible in the sky after the Full Moon – known as *waning*. As the Moon wanes, so the influence of these things in your life can wane.

The Waning Moon is the period between the Full and New Moons. This phase of the Moon is powerful for working on things you want less of or that you want to banish from your life.

Rituals for letting go are best done during the Full or Waning Moon phases.

Even if you don't want to start coordinating your rituals and spellwork with the Moon, it is worth your time to start paying attention to where She is in Her cycle at any given time. Just this little bit of awareness can help you reconnect to the wilder parts of you. While you may not find yourself running through the woods howling under the Full Moon with a pack of your best friends (true story), taking time to gaze at the Moon helps us remember that we are part of all that is.

Of course, feel free to howl.

The Wheel of the Year

The second sacred calendar used by many Feminist Witches is known as the Wheel of the Year, and has much in common with the Wiccan sacred calendar. The biggest difference is that the Wiccan calendar is based around the veneration of a God and a Goddess, and the cycle tells the story of their coming together. Feminist Witchcraft rituals around these seasonal holidays instead focus just on the Goddess as She works through the cycle of the seasons which mirror the cycles of life. Specific Goddess stories and myths may be associated with these holidays as well. The Wheel of the Year is said to be drawn from European agricultural calendars of the distant past, but it's hard to evaluate these claims. I tend to think of them as a modern interpretation of the agrarian cycle, and to find more meaning in them as reflections of the stages and cycles of life.

There are eight sacred days, sometimes called *Sabbats*, in the Wheel of the Year. They are:

- **Samhain** (*sow-when*), October 31 (Northern Hemisphere)/ May 1 (Southern Hemisphere). This is a feast to honor the dead and to mark the passage of the old year into the new year. Rituals of remembrance, of collective mourning, and of contemplation are common. Many Feminist Witches honor Dark Goddesses such as Hecate or Hel at this time.

- **Yule/Winter Solstice**, December 21 (NH)/June 21 (SH). Sometimes known as Midwinter, this holiday marks the deepest point of winter. Rituals and celebrations around community, maintaining hope in the dark, and celebrating the returning Sun are common.
- **Imbolc/Brighid**, February 1 (NH)/August 1 (SH). A celebration of the first stirrings of spring and of life, this holiday marks the slow emergence into the new year. Sacred to Brighid, Irish Goddess of smithcraft, poetry, and healing, this is a great time to set intentions about creative projects for the next year.
- **Ostara/Spring Equinox**, March 21 (NH)/September 21 (SH). The official start of spring! The earth comes alive, and we come alive with it. Now is the time we take concrete action on those intentions we set at Imbolc.
- **Beltaine**, May 1 (NH)/October 31 (SH). This holiday honors the fertility of the late spring. It is an ideal time to do work around abundance (including physical fertility) in your life. Beltaine festivals have been known to be among the most raucous!
- **Litha/Summer Solstice**, June 21 (NH)/December 21 (SH). The longest day and shortest night mean that the year is turning. At this point, we begin thinking of the coming of the winter and what we will harvest in the coming months. A wonderful community celebration time, but also a time to check and be honest with yourself about the intentions you set and your progress on projects. Weed things out accordingly.
- **Lammas/Lughnasadh**, August 1 (NH)/February 1 (SH). The first harvest. This is a time to honor the hard work

you've done that has started to show fruit. Rituals around communal meals are common at this time.

- **Mabon/Fall Equinox**, September 21 (NH)/March 21 (SH). The Fall Equinox marks the last point on the Wheel before Samhain returns again. Here we celebrate our harvest, our accomplishments for the year. We also start to think about what we will take with us into the dark half of the year, what we will work on and how we will care for ourselves and others.

Celebrating the Wheel of the Year can feel a little odd in the modern world, where most of us do not harvest or butcher our own food. And those of us living in regions where the cycle of the seasons does not map onto the Wheel may very well find it hard to resonate with the agrarian themes (take it from me, I have done a Yule ritual in Texas when it was 70 degrees on the day of the Solstice). In Feminist Witchcraft, we're encouraged to dive into the metaphor and instead see the Wheel as reflective of the various stages we go through in our lives, whether annually or in our lifetime. By making these stages into something to be honored and made sacred, we are better able to see the sacred within ourselves and feel our connection to everything that lives, every has lived, ever will live.

Chapter 9

Witchcraft for the Revolution

Our whirlwind journey through the basics of Feminist Witchcraft is nearly at its end, which means that soon you'll be venturing onto your own witchy path. I hope that what I have set down here has been and will be helpful as you step into your power and find the Witch and the Goddess within.

I have not infrequently been asked, especially in the age of Instagrammable Witchcraft, if all this isn't simply self-indulgence, a way to feel like I'm powerful and making a difference in the world without actually having to risk anything. While I understand where that question comes from, my answer is a resounding *No*. Are there folks out there who call themselves Witches – even Feminist Witches – and who never take a concrete action towards a better world, instead focusing on their crystal collection or latest $5000 retreat? Sure there are. I've met them. But there are also many more people who are dedicated to the path of Feminist Witchcraft as a path of personal healing *and* a path towards a more just, more healed, and more equitable world.

Way back at the beginning of this book, I recalled a mentor who told me that healing myself would be the most important step I'd take on my journey into Feminist Craft. From the outside, especially to those who do not suffer the worst of patriarchy's violence, taking time to heal oneself through ritual, meditation, bodywork, community building, and therapy can look very much like self-indulgence. But within the worldview of Feminist Witchcraft, it is an act of resistance and of taking back power. Those of us who have been most profoundly wounded by patriarchy know that the greatest casualty of patriarchal violence is being cut off from our own power, our own worth, our own sacredness. When we reclaim these things, we not only become more powerful agents of change in the world at large, but we also show *other people who have been wounded by patriarchy that healing is possible*. We go on to create spaces, projects, art, scholarship, and communities that operate by different rules and disrupt the patriarchal status quo. That is the opposite of self-involved or self-indulgent.

One of the greatest lessons that Feminist Witchcraft has taught me is that when we heal ourselves, we become more able to heal the world. And that might not mean doing the spell that puts an end to police brutality or world hunger. Instead it might mean becoming an advocate for one person who is struggling through the system. Or to create the full moon circle that allows women and others wounded by patriarchy to tell their stories, to realize they are not alone, and to organize for collective action based on that knowledge. The healing we do for ourselves, the empowerment we find, the connection we find with the Sacred and with others, all ripple out into the world.

I am not naive enough to believe that if we all just meditated under the Full Moon or light the right candles or licked the right crystals, the ills of settler colonialism, late-stage capitalism, all the -isms one can think of, and climate change will disappear. But I do believe that each of us that claims our power, who says *no* to simply going along with things as they have always been done, who reaches a hand out to another, who dares to say *This is wrong* in the face of injustice, helps us move toward the world we want to live in.

As I finish this book, our planet is in grave danger from man-made climate change, from the rise of fascism worldwide, from wars with weapons that wreak great destruction, from political division and rising tides of political violence. It is easy to feel hopeless. It is easy to be afraid.

- I am not hopeless. I am not afraid.
- We stand in a place between the worlds.
- What is between the worlds can change the worlds.
- *And what can change the worlds is US.*

Endnotes

1. I use the spelling *magick*, in line with many other writers on metaphysical topics, to differentiate from stage magic or sleight of hand.
2. *Cisgender* means that a person identifies with the gender assigned to them at birth/that was assumed of them at birth.
3. I use the term *enabled* to indicate that, at this point in my life anyway, I do not navigate the world as a person with one or more disabilities.
4. Starhawk, 1979 *The Spiral Dance: The Rebirth of the Ancient Religion of the Great Goddess* (Harper)
5. A full discussion of the uses of witchcraft across cultures is far beyond the scope of this volume. There is a rich anthropological literature on witchcraft in various cultures, as well as a healthy corpus of literature written by practitioners themselves, that can help put witchcraft-as-resistance into a larger context. I encourage readers interested in learning more about this aspect of witchcraft writ large to explore the resources at the end of this book.
6. Patricia Hopkins and Sherry Ruth Anderson, *The Feminine Face of God: The Unfolding of the Sacred in Women* (Bantam, 1992).
7. This term was coined by Goddess scholar Carol P. Christ and is a feminization of *theology*.
8. Daly, along with several other Feminist Spirituality and Feminist Witchcraft writers and thinkers I will reference in this chapter, have a number of troubling and bigoted views on the inclusion of transgender women within "women's spaces." I disagree vehemently with their exclusionary views, as I will discuss later in this book. I find it necessary to ground any discussion of the history of Feminist Witchcraft in the context of these writers

even while I reject many of their positions and beliefs. I footnote these as necessary so readers can make choices about which primary sources to engage with in depth.

9. I recognize that anyone of any gender can practice Feminist Witchcraft, though I argue that those who are used to having their own genders centered in the dominant culture may struggle with a shift in paradigm. I have chosen to talk in terms of women here because that is in line with the paradigm of Feminist Craft as it was founded. Also, to be clear, my use of *women* includes both cis and trans women.
10. Cynthia Eller, *The Myth of Matriarchal Prehistory: Why an Invented Past Won't Give Women a Future* (Beacon, 2001).
11. I mean this in the most basic sense – that my body is a woman's body because I am a woman. I do not subscribe to the idea held by many early (and some contemporary) Feminist Witches that a woman's body is only a body that contains a uterus and ovaries.
12. By *cis-centric,* I mean that it centered the experiences of cisgender women and excluded the experiences of trans women through erasure. *Cis-normative* means that these writers write as though the experiences of cisgender people are the natural and normal condition for humans. Some of these writers go on to explicitly include trans women from the discussion. Those who do not (and who have not since come out with trans exclusionary views) are best seen as a product of their time and of the prevailing language being used.
13. I use the term *brave space* rather than *safe space* intentionally, here and in my circles. Brave spaces are an idea born out of Black Feminist writings, especially those of bell hooks and Patricia Hill Collins. A brave space is a space in which people are encouraged and supported in taking appropriate risks, being vulnerable, and asking hard questions.

14. This is adapted from the work of Starhawk in *The Spiral Dance* (1979). I have previously used her original version, which references "warm womb waters," but worked with my circle to adapt it for a more gender-inclusive version. My gratitude for this and many other things in my practice goes to Starhawk.
15. I first heard this from the priestess who wrote it at a large Pagan festival in Texas around 1999. I have used and loved it ever since. Barb, wherever you are, thank you.

Recommended Readings and Resources

Foundational Texts in Feminist Spirituality and Feminist Witchcraft

Please note that a number (though not all) of the authors listed below have espoused bioessentialist or otherwise problematic views. They are still important for understanding the history of these two intertwined spiritual movements, but should be approached critically.

Budapest, Z. 1989 *The Holy Book of Women's Mysteries* (HarperOne)

Budapest, Z. 1989 *The Grandmother of Time: A Woman's Book of Celebrations, Spells, and Sacred Objects for Every Month of the Year* (HarperOne)

Budapest, Z. 1991 *Grandmother Moon: Lunar Magic in Our Lives – Spells, Rituals, Goddesses, Legends, and Emotions Under the Moon* (HarperOne)

Christ, Carol P. 1978 "Why Women Need the Goddess" *Heresies: The Great Goddess Issue* Access via https://www.goddessariadne.org/why-women-need-the-goddess-part-1

Daly, Mary 1973 *Beyond God the Father: Toward a Philosophy of Women's Liberation* (Beacon)

Greenfield, Trevor, ed. 2014 *Naming the Goddess* (Moon Books)

Greenfield, Trevor, ed. 2016 *The Goddess in America: The Divine Feminine in Cultural Context* (Moon Books)

Greenfield, Trevor, ed. 2018 *Seven Ages of the Goddess* (Moon Books)

Mountainwater, Shekinah 1991 *Ariadne's Thread: A Workbook of Goddess Magic* (Crossing Press)

Radford Ruether, Rosemary 1983 *Sexism and God-Talk: Toward a Feminist Theology* (Beacon)

Radford Ruether, Rosemary 1994 *Gaia and God: An Ecofeminist Theology of Earth Healing* (HarperOne)

Starhawk 1979 *The Spiral Dance: The Rebirth of the Ancient Religion of the Great Goddess* (HarperOne)
Stein, Diane and Page Smith 1986 *The Women's Spirituality Book* (Llewellyn)
Stein, Diane 1990 *All Women are Healers: A Comprehensive Guide to Natural Healing* (Crossing Press)
Stein, Diane 1991 *Casting the Circle: A Woman's Book of Ritual* (Crossing Press)

MOON BOOKS

PAGANISM & SHAMANISM

What is Paganism? A religion, a spirituality, an alternative belief system, nature worship? You can fi nd support for all these definitions (and many more) in dictionaries, encyclopaedias, and text books of religion, but subscribe to any one and the truth will evade you. Above all Paganism is a creative pursuit, an encounter with reality, an exploration of meaning and an expression of the soul. Druids, Heathens, Wiccans and others, all contribute their insights and literary riches to the Pagan tradition. Moon Books invites you to begin or to deepen your own encounter, right here, right now.

If you have enjoyed this book, why not tell other readers by posting a review on your preferred book site.

Bestsellers from Moon Books
Pagan Portals Series

The Morrigan

Meeting the Great Queens

Morgan Daimler

Ancient and enigmatic, the Morrigan reaches out to us. On shadowed wings and in raven's call, meet the ancient Irish goddess of war, battle, prophecy, death, sovereignty, and magic.

Paperback: 978-1-78279-833-0 ebook: 978-1-78279-834-7

The Awen Alone

Walking the Path of the Solitary Druid

Joanna van der Hoeven

An introductory guide for the solitary Druid, The Awen Alone will accompany you as you explore, and seek out your own place within the natural world.

Paperback: 978-1-78279-547-6 ebook: 978-1-78279-546-9

Moon Magic

Rachel Patterson

An introduction to working with the phases of the Moon, what they are and how to live in harmony with the lunar year and to utilise all the magical powers it provides.

Paperback: 978-1-78279-281-9 ebook: 978-1-78279-282-6

Hekate

A Devotional

Vivienne Moss

Hekate, Queen of Witches and the Shadow-Lands, haunts the pages of this devotional bringing magic and enchantment into your lives.

Paperback: 978-1-78535-161-7 ebook: 978-1-78535-162-4

Bestsellers from Moon Books

Keeping Her Keys

An Introduction to Hekate's Modern Witchcraft

Cyndi Brannen

Blending Hekate, witchcraft and personal development together to create a powerful new magickal perspective.

Paperback: 978-1-78904-075-3 ebook 978-1-78904-076-0

Journey to the Dark Goddess

How to Return to Your Soul

Jane Meredith

Discover the powerful secrets of the Dark Goddess and transform your depression, grief and pain into healing and integration.

Paperback: 978-1-84694-677-6 ebook: 978-1-78099-223-5

Shamanic Reiki

Expanded Ways of Working with Universal Life Force Energy

Llyn Roberts, Robert Levy

Shamanism and Reiki are each powerful ways of healing; together, their power multiplies. Shamanic Reiki introduces techniques to help healers and Reiki practitioners tap ancient healing wisdom.

Paperback: 978-1-84694-037-8 ebook: 978-1-84694-650-9

Southern Cunning

Folkloric Witchcraft in the American South

Aaron Oberon

Modern witchcraft with a Southern flair, this book is a journey through the folklore of the American South and a look at the power these stories hold for modern witches.

Paperback: 978-1-78904-196-5 ebook: 978-1-78904-197-2